CROSSROADS

A Memoir

ELLIE CONNELLY

Order this book online at www.trafford.com
or email orders@trafford.com

Most Trafford titles are also available at major online book retailers.

Printed in the United States of America.

ISBN: 978-1-4907-4833-7 (sc)
ISBN: 978-1-4907-4835-1 (hc)
ISBN: 978-1-4907-4834-4 (e)

Library of Congress Control Number: 2014917768

Trafford rev. 01/13/2015

 www.trafford.com

North America & international
toll-free: 1 888 232 4444 (USA & Canada)
fax: 812 355 4082

DEDICATION

To my Victoria, my Sophia, my Lorraine and lastly my Julia
To the four strongest women in my life.
I am honored to call you friend.
I thank you for being the most intricate and most
beautiful branches on my tree, and for growing and
standing with me through all the storms of my life.

To My Children

⸻❖⸻

I thank God everyday that he let me experience the joy of motherhood. I never knew complete love, until each of you was born. I love each and every one of you with every part of me. I loved the babies I cared for, the children I grew with, but mostly the people you are today. You are not just branches. You are my foundation and have given me the strength to weather the storms. I truly love all of you.

Special Thanks

Samantha Elphick
For making my words come to life and
letting me fulfill my dream.

Contents

Foreword xiii

Chapter One: Childhood 1
Chapter Two: Adolescence 7
Chapter Three: High School 18
Chapter Four: Breaking Away 34
Chapter Five: Wedded Bliss 40
Chapter Six: Revelations 50
Chapter Seven: Self Reliance 71
Chapter Eight: Uncommitted 82
Chapter Nine: Deception - Joe 90
Chapter Ten: Immorality 101
Chapter Eleven: Intrigue 120
Chapter Twelve: Dream Land 136
Chapter Thirteen: The Storm 153
Chapter Fourteen: The Aftermath 164
Chapter Fifteen: Vivified 179
Chapter Sixteen: Happily Never After 189
Chapter Seventeen: Humility – Adversity – Tragedy 205
Chapter Eighteen: My Awakening 216

FOREWORD

Years ago I wrote a poem to a very special person. I called it *My Tree of Life.* It may shed some light on a deeper understanding of the life journey I am about to write.

I pictured myself growing like the Maple tree, with vibrant red leaves, tall and straight up into the sky. But instead, I became more like the Oak tree, not straight and tall, but short and wide. Some of the branches were mangled and twisted, while others grew towards the ground or simply broke away and died. New branches replaced the old. Exactly what happens in our life? My big, strong trunk always had moss growing on it, but looking at this tree it was unique and fascinating, unlike other trees. All the details of growth during the years in this tree are my memories within. Right at the top of this tree, there is new foliage with strong growth. Three very strong branches have begun to grow towards the sky, spurting new buds as each branch appears.

The Oak tree still stands strong after all the storms, droughts and sunshine, waiting for whatever comes next, hoping for a few sunny days. I have gone all around in my life with lovers, husbands, friends and my children to end up the same as I started — alone, with no one to love, or care for me. So yes, the Crossroads of my life are about my greatest memories. Many people have loved me and even though they may not have lasted, at least I have those years and memories. So here I am still standing five and three quarter inches tall, I'll never be as tall as the Maple tree I dreamed of, but I am strong like the Oak tree and my branches continue to grow . . .

"Parents can only give good advice or put them on the right path, but the final forming of a person's character lies in their own hands."

— Anne Frank

CHAPTER ONE

CHILDHOOD

I came from a troubled home, but it's the only home I knew. Sure, growing up I looked at my friends' families and could see that we were all different in some way or another. Isn't that what we are supposed to be—individuals? Yes, I had friends that I wished their parents were mine, but on the other hand I had friends whose parents were more messed up then mine. I soon came to the conclusion that I was fine with the ones I had. Actually, what else can you do? Your family is your family forever, and sometimes that doesn't seem quite fair. We don't pick our family or our roots. Don't waste your energy on what you could have had, spend time on what you have and value. You just may be surprised.

Take me for instance. The troubled family I grew up with did have its perks. We lived on Staten Island and my grandparents lived in Manhattan, for as long as I can remember, every Friday mom took us to catch the big ferry to Manhattan. On Sunday nights my father would come and pick us up, we always had a blast on those weekends. Sometimes mom didn't stay, so my siblings and I got to be alone with our wonderful grandparents. In a way I feel lucky that my family was so dysfunctional, because we never had to stay home on weekends like a happy little family. From an early age I knew I wasn't loved. I never seemed to fit in with my family, but it wasn't all that bad, God gave me my Nanny, and she loved me.

My grandparents lived in a two-bedroom, public housing apartment in Manhattan. Every weekend my siblings and I would fill up that apartment with happiness and laughter. I remember how Nanny would hug me so tight and she would place her arms around me with her chin pressing down on my head. I don't recall her ever saying that she loved me until years later, but boy I always felt her love. I was with my Nanny every weekend, school holidays, and summer vacations until I was thirteen-years-old. My grandfather was the sweetest, kindest man I ever knew. He had his problems, but as a young girl I only ever saw a man who loved his little granddaughter. Just by looking into their faces, I could see the happiness I brought into their lives just by walking through the door.

My parents were married at seventeen. They were children having children, all born one year apart. My sister Marion was one year older, and my brother Mikie, was one year younger. My father worked in his family's painting business and my mom was what you called in those days—a housewife. After eight years, Nicky my brother came along unexpectedly. My family relocated many times causing me to attend four different grammar schools, two junior high schools and then a high school, which I attended when my parents purchased their first home. The only stability I had in those years was my grandparents, going there was paradise to me.

My story is one of growing up in two very different worlds. I have the not-so-good memories with my parents at home, and then the memories of my grandparents and friends in the city. I lived as two different people. In my grandparents' home there was no arguing, no meanness, just love. Then there was Danny, he lived in Manhattan and became my constant friend. He was a skinny little kid who suffered with asthma. Being one of a twin, and the sickly one, his brother was naturally smarter, taller, and stronger. His mother and my Nanny were best friends so for as long as I can remember, it was always Danny and me. He was my New York friend on weekends and vacations. We played every card game imaginable, board games, watched old movies, and he would even play with my Barbie and Ken dolls with me.

With Danny suffering from asthma, it prevented us from doing a lot of physical activities, but we had so much fun doing other things. My Manhattan friends were Danny, Kevin, James, Frankie, Tito and Manuel. Yes, you got it - all boys! I liked playing with the boys. Summertime was opening up the hydrant pumps, wrapping cardboard around our waists sitting in front excitedly waiting for our friends to release the big gush of water, pushing us across the street while we laughed hysterically. I became a novelty, everyone waited for my arrival on weekends, and they treated me very special. We would play in the park by the East Side River, and on a few occasions we would even dive into the gunky water.

Life with my family was very different, being told every day that you never fit in, one sadly gets to believe that, especially when you have a sister one year older, but so much taller. Here is an example, when she made her communion in the first grade, her communion dress didn't fit me until I was in the fifth grade. Today she is 5'7. I am 5' ¾" and my brother Mikie is 6'1. I was constantly teased from age four. I was always told to "grow up" and called a whiner or piss eyes. My sister was more like a mother, always repeating the things that I did wrong. I can't recall one time when my sister talked to me, other than to make fun of me. Her job was to take care of Mikie and me. She sure didn't enjoy being a first grader having to take her sister to the bus for kindergarten. Looking back she never got to be a child, and instead she took on the role of being a mommy.

And as for me, I was just the opposite. I wanted to be a child, I loved running, the outdoors, riding bikes, playing football, wrestling with the boys. Yet, I also loved being a little girl playing make believe with my dolls, and when I was older I only played with my Barbie dolls at Nanny's house. This became my secret world that I only let Danny share with me.

In second grade we moved to St. George. That was where my other boy crew lived. When I grew up I had no parental supervision. I would wake up, go out to play, come home for lunch, and then back again for dinner. We were street kids coming up with games and adventures everyday. We had no toys to play with, for that was a time when kids became inventive and used their imagination. I was the tomboy and loved playing with the boys. I never told these boys I played with dolls. We would climb trees, play football, compete in races. I was really fast for a girl. Two of them had sisters a year younger than me. We played together, but it wasn't like playing with the boys—girlfriends are too stressful. All they do is care about their looks and outfits. They gossip about friends behind their backs and I didn't like that. With the boys we always had an adventure, we talked but never about anything personal. My favorite was playing football. They would fight to have me on their team, which I thought was pretty cool. We fought a lot and looking back I stood up for myself pretty good—wrestling on the ground, punching and kicking each other. Some of boys were faster than me, when they would tease me they quickly ran away. I would take off my shoe and throw it, always hitting my target in the head. But the next day we were friends again. When you fight with a girl she runs home crying to mommy, and girls hold grudges for days.

My friends and I laughed a lot. We would get into trouble, but not about anything malicious. It was more about getting dirty and my mother hated that.

"Why can't you be like Marion?" she would ask, but I dug my heels in deeper. Darn it! I wasn't Marion I was Ellie! I never let them change me to be what they wanted. She and my mother always reassured me that the boys were only my friends and I did not have a boy who loved me like Marion. I was only seven-years-old. They would also say that she was grandpa's favorite, but that didn't faze me because I knew that I had my Nanny.

By the time I was seven, my young brother, Mikie, was babied by my mom and told every day how handsome he was. Marion was beautiful and also told that every day and as for me.

"Why do you dress like that, or why can't you act like a girl?" was all I heard. We lived in pretty close quarters and were lucky that my father was handy in construction. He was able to divide a room for my sister and me, and then he made a partition for my brother on the other side of the room. I remember having a blackboard on the back of my bedroom door. One night I wrote on it NOBODY LOVES ME!

No one even asked who had written that. They all knew my handwriting, yet it saddened me no one had responded to my little message. I was seven, alone, and no one cared. One time I was attacked by a dog, I could not have been more than ten-years-old. I came into the apartment screaming and crying, blood was all over me, but my mother quickly smacked me across the face.

"Calm down," she yelled, I was shocked. Then she took me to the hospital where I received over twenty stitches on my arms and stomach. But, when a stupid icicle fell and hit my sister on the head, I remember mom comforting her hysteria, telling her everything would be all right. I could never understand why they didn't like me. I had friends whose parents were mean, but they were mean to all their children.

We moved out of St. George and my parents rented my grandmother's house. I was in the sixth grade and went to school every day without lunch or lunch money. During the lunchtime hour I would walk around because I was too embarrassed for the kids to see that I didn't have any. One girl in my class would sometimes invite me to her house for lunch. One day I was called down to the office, and to my surprise my mother was sitting there. I was asked where I had gone for lunch. I told them that I was walking on the Blvd.

Boy, they reprimanded my mother that day, and you guessed it . . . I got into real big trouble when I got home. It was Marion's job to make sure we had lunch, not my mother's. Same year on Valentines Day, a huge fight broke out between my mom, dad and Alice (my mom's friend). My father came home with candy and flowers for my mom, and she immediately threw them at Alice.

"Give them to your fucking girlfriend," she roared at him.

All hell broke loose, my father immediately pulled my mom off Alice and then she started attacking him. My father had always cheated on my mother. I grew up hearing words like: whore, douchebag or tramp. I felt bad for my mother, as I was old enough now to know how he had hurt her. She was proud of finally standing up for herself. A few days later my mom had given me a note to give to my teacher, my teacher hugged me and I had no idea why. When I came home from school there was a moving van in front of the house it was Friday. On Monday I went to a new school.

———————

CHAPTER TWO

ADOLESCENCE

W e moved to the Fox Hill section of Staten Island, I went to the public school for six months. I didn't make any friends at that school, but then in September I attended junior high. I was put in the slower classes with other students one could only describe as animals. My reading class consisted of three girls and eighteen boys—they were bad. When I would pass by them they would pull up my dress and continually tease me, it was insane.

I hated the class. I met one girl and her name was Beverly, we became good friends and maintained some sanity. Beverly didn't live near me so I couldn't hang with her. After being in this class for about a month, there was one boy who wouldn't leave her alone. He always made her cry, so I jumped on him and started beating him up. After that, any boy who bothered us, I would beat up right there in class. I was sent to the Dean's office almost every day. I liked being a tomboy. I found a group of about twelve boys, we loved to climb trees, and over the months we built a tree house together. We would steal the wood from a lumberyard, nails from a local store, and one of the guys brought his dad's tools. We were so proud when it was finished and it turned out to be very large.

One day someone was throwing out a small couch. I remember taking it to our tree house, we all just stood there looking and thinking, none of us spoke, as we were all trying to figure out how we could get it up there. Finally, we came up with a crazy idea—two boys went up in the tree house, two others remained at the bottom. We lifted the couch and placed the bottom feet on the steps, we slid it up the stairs by placing pieces of wood under the couch and pushing it up until the boys at the top were able to grab it. It took a lot of doing but we had a couch in our tree house, we were so proud of ourselves, and we did it with one try!

When I was home through the week that summer, my friends and I would go to Brady's pond. We were not allowed to go there, but nonetheless we were there every day. We hung a rope from a tree, jumped onto the rope, making sure that our hands and feet held on tight while swinging out over the lake, and then jumped off. What fun, I just didn't want to grow up.

MY FIRST KISS

One day I went back to St. George to visit my old friends and everything had changed. The boys I used to play with were now into sex and girls. They had a clubhouse with a television, sofa, and chairs. Sean was one of the guys, and he was the cutest boy in the world. A few years back we were playing seven minutes in heaven (all the girls loved Sean) they would tell me that he kissed them. I had a secret crush on him and got so excited when the coin landed on me. That meant we were going to be alone for seven minutes. Sean was going to kiss me, and I was ready. But, that didn't happen. I was about ten-years-old. We went into the bathroom, but he didn't kiss me. Instead, he took out toothpaste and began squirting it to make a sound like he was on the toilet. He messed around doing boy stuff. I just laughed and laughed. I guess boys just didn't see me as a real girl.

I hadn't seen Sean for two years, now he was cuter than ever. His eyes were gorgeous and had a devilish sparkle. We were going to watch "To Sir with Love". He sat on a chair and asked me to sit beside him. He held my hand and then it finally happened— he kissed me, and then we tongue kissed. It was such a strange feeling, but it felt wonderful. The year before I had gone out with my cousin Allie, and a friend of hers had tried to tongue kiss me. It was disgusting, but this was different. It was soft and gentle and I liked it very much. We watched the movie and loved it. Now I was Sean's girlfriend, we were so excited because in September he was going to be in my school again. We were the same age, but he was a year behind me. My parents didn't like me going back to St. George, so it was hard for us to see each other. Sean never did go to my school, and after a few weeks I heard that he had moved in with his father on Long Island. I felt lost. That was my last year hanging out with boys, because at the end of the summer, I had become a woman.

BECOMING A WOMAN

I grew up with so many inferiority complexes because in my home every insult was done in a joking manner. Ellie didn't get her period. Ellie doesn't have boobs. Why is Ellie wearing a training bra? She doesn't have any boobs. Or they would say things like.

"Your nose is like a ski slope, and little ants could race down your nose, when are you going to grow?"

I remember the summer I became a lady. I tried to keep it from everyone, but Nanny had found the bloodstains on my panties. She came into the bedroom and softly told me what she had seen. She asked me gently if I had gotten my period. I nodded and begged her not to tell anyone. I guess Nanny did the right thing by telling my mom, but knowing how my family was, she should have kept my secret.

At this age I always went to Manhattan by myself, so when I came home my father, my uncle Willie, and my godfather Robert were in the house. As soon as I opened the door they all started cheering.

"Yeah, yeah, yeah, Ellie finally got it! She finally got her period."

My Uncle Willie would tease me.

"Come here and let me see what a woman looks like?"

I was shocked. But, the worst thing was to see my mother laughing out loud with them. I started crying and ran into my room. Then I heard my father.

"There goes piss eyes and she can't even take a joke," he sneered.

I hated them, I hated all of them, and wished I could live with Nanny, but my mother wouldn't let me.

Well, I got my period, but didn't grow boobs. I didn't grow any taller either and mother could not understand this. It was as if I was a mutant in her beautiful family. That year I measured myself every day at school. I wanted so desperately to be 5 feet 1 inch. That wasn't a hard goal. I didn't want to be as big as my sister I just wanted to reach 5 feet 1 inch. Sadly, it never happened, I stayed at 5 ¾ inches even to this day.

Within the first couple of weeks into the eighth grade school year, there was this tall Russian girl who kept picking on me in the lunchroom. I refused to fight in school so we set a fight location up in my apartment complex. All the kids were in a circle and the Russian girl and I were in the middle. I remember standing and looking at her, she had to be at least 5 feet 9 inches tall. I remember thinking that if I punched her I would only reach her shoulder.

Suddenly, she pushed me, and with my left hand I impulsively took off my shoe and I hit her in the head. Then with my right hand I punched her on the side of her face and she fell down. I needed to get her on the ground. Once she was down, I jumped on top of her and started punching. Back then if your opponent says *enough,* the fight is over. We never beat anyone like you see kids do today. It was a fight, giving a few punches, kicks and sometimes bites. We always fought one on one. Cha Cha, one of the girls who had been watching the fight, came over to me.

"Ellie, you are one tough bitch," she grinned. After that our friendship began.

CHRISTMAS TIME

This particular Christmas I wanted to do something special for my mom. She loved to shop and buy beautiful clothes. She had a favorite store called Ruby Lane in Stapleton. I went to the store and picked out a pair of silk black slacks and a white silk, ruffled blouse. I put them on lay-a-way and went to the store daily with my lunch money. I took $1 and walked there every day after school, because otherwise I was afraid I would spend it. I couldn't wait to see mom's face when she opened it. She would know how much I loved her.

Well, my parents were still apart and it was two days before Christmas. I showed Marion what I had bought my mom and she asked me about a present for dad. I had no more money to buy my father anything. Marion convinced me that we should put both of our names on their presents. My father slept over that night, and Christmas morning finally arrived. I was so excited I didn't even care what I got for Christmas. I just wanted my mother to open her present. Then I saw the face I was waiting for, the one that showed me she loved it. She opened the box.

"Oh, this is so beautiful. It must have been expensive. I can't wait to put them on. I think I'll wear this outfit for New Year's Eve." I was beaming listening to her comments. I felt happy that I had finally done something right. Then my whole world crumbled when I heard.

"Oh Marion, it's beautiful, thank you so much," she said, and hugged her.

My sister didn't tell her that I had bought it.

"Mom, I knew you would like it," I heard her say. Mom casually thanked me as if I had nothing to do with it. Why would she think that her tomboy daughter could pick out something so beautiful? I don't know whom I was madder at, my mother or my sister for not saying anything.

MY FIRST SLEEP OVER

This was a good year for me for I was having my first birthday party at home—a sleep over with five girlfriends. Every year I had spent my birthday with my grandparents during the Christmas break. I would always get my present on my sister's birthday (21st of December) even though my birthday was at the end of the year. Sometimes my mother wasn't even there for my birthday, as she usually went out for New Year's Eve with my father.

My mother and sister had gone out. Mom left frozen pizzas for us, but when I heated up the oven, I suddenly smelt something weird. I realized the iron was in the oven, and of course it had melted. I immediately took it out and placed it in the sink. Then I put the pizza in to heat while my friends and I were dancing to music. My mother returned.

"What is that smell? You fucking idiot you burned the iron!" she yelled, right there in front of everyone. She not only screamed at me, but when I answered her back she smacked me in front of everyone.

"You are just a fucking moron. You are never going to grow up!" She screamed at me viciously. I was so embarrassed and my friends remained silent, they were in shock. The worst of it all was that Marion kept repeating my mother's abusive words. That night I decided that was it for me, I was done. No more. I knew nothing I ever did would be right, and I stopped trying to please them. I lived with them, but I certainly didn't like any of them. My mother had never tendered to me, loved me, or respected me as her daughter. To this day I never understood why, but some things in life are there to make us strong. I was determined not to become my family.

BREAKING AWAY

This was the year I truly broke away from my family. My school was interracial. I don't know if it was because of zoning changes, but by eighth grade there were not many white children in the school. My best friend was Cha Cha, and she was half black. My parents did not approve of her. She was my friend and opened a new world for me. Her mother was French and Cha Cha lived with her mom and stepdad. I didn't get to meet her real dad for six months.

Cha Cha and I loved to shoplift. We were great at it. We had a system all worked out. We would go in the store wearing a poncho. We always bought something very cheap so that we had a bag from that store. Sometimes we would leave with eight outfits hidden underneath. After stealing some items, we would then go back in and return what we could to get money for the items. Then we would shop for things we liked. Cha Cha and I wore matching outfits— black high top sneakers, with boy's high white socks and black stripes. We wore brown leather wraparound mini skirts that closed with only two clasps at the top. We would wear shorts underneath our skirts. We thought we were cool, but my mother hated the look.

No longer climbing trees, my tomboy days were behind me. I was the only person in the group who was white. There were so many of us, I can only recall a few names. We loved to fight. That was common back then, and it felt good being on the other end. I had been beat up so much in the past. Cha Cha said that I was an easy target because I was so small. When we weren't fighting we were dancing. I loved music. When there were no parties going on we would listen to a little portable radio, learning the moves of the current dances in someone's apartment or just sitting on the stoop.

"You have to have some black in you girl because you have soul," they would tell me. Soul Train was our favorite show to watch. I was their soul sister and that's what they called me. I was in a different world, a tougher world, but we all looked out for each other. The girls usually fought over the boys, just like all girls. The boys were really nice to me. Two were my favorites, Chandler and Terrell. Chandler lived in my building and he was like Cha Cha, but his mom was black and his dad white. I would talk to Terrell all the time. He was a great dancer and we danced together a lot.

When he tried to kiss me, I told him that I only liked him as a friend. Some of the girls heard about this and accused me of being prejudiced. They ordered me to kiss Terrell by the end of the school day, and if I didn't they were going to beat me up. I wasn't prejudice, but I didn't like Terrell that way. I wasn't having anyone tell me what I had to do. I went to the nurse's office and told her that I didn't feel well and was sent home.

My parents were prejudice and I knew they would do something about this. I told my mother what happened and I was immediately transferred to a new junior high school. I never said goodbye to any of my friends, because I didn't know who was still my friend. The area had changed and within a month, we moved into my father's parent's house, but unfortunately this didn't work out.

THE BEST TIME IN MY LIFE

My parents decided to buy a home. My mom was going to school to become a beautician. We lived apart so the family could save money for a down payment. To my delight, I moved with my mother, brothers Mikie and Nicky, into Nanny's house. Marion and my father lived in Staten Island. This was probably the best time of my life. I had to travel far to get to school. I took buses on the Manhattan side, the Ferry and then one bus on Staten Island.

But, this was the year I met Becky, she was in most of my classes. As soon as we saw each other the feeling was mutual. From the first day in school she became my friend.

Danny met me every day at the bus stop on the Manhattan side. My whole life I never had anyone waiting for me, and this felt so good. When I would arrive home, Nanny and Grandpa would always have a snack waiting for me. We also had a puppy and I named him, Boo Boo. This was a happy time.

At this age I was experimenting and drugs were everywhere. My friends and I would hang out, and my favorite thing to do was to sniff glue. One day I cut school and went down to the beach to sniff glue. I got so stoned that I fell asleep. The glue was all over my face. I remember going home picking off the glue, but when I got off the bus Danny wanted to know what happened to my eyebrows?" I had plucked then all out. I told the family that I shaved them because I didn't like them.

After the glue incident, I didn't want to hang out with those kids anymore—I was afraid of some of them. Becky didn't do drugs and I believe that God sent her to me. Becky had black hair and brown eyes, she dressed like a boy and seemed so much tougher than me, but in actuality Becky didn't have a mean bone in her body. We were the outcasts of our families and it was okay now because I finally had a sister, someone who thought like me, dressed like me, smoked like me, and cursed liked me.

Becky and I were nuts, we would fill our mouths up with water from the school fountain and chase each other through the halls, spitting the water at each other. One day I spat the water on the Vice Principal, he had walked out of the classroom at the exact time the water released from my mouth. Becky could have run away, but instead she stayed and we were punished together. I could always make Becky laugh, and she would always get in trouble. I used to blow my nose real loud, it sounded like a foghorn, in Science class. Becky knew I was fooling around, but the teacher and the other children had no idea. Becky would always get into trouble for laughing. In September I was moving to South Beach and I was going to be living right around the corner from Becky. We were so excited.

SUMMER IN THE CITY
This summer everything changed involving hormones and sex. I was still living at Nanny's. The girls were calling me a tramp because I hung out with the boys. I finally met one girl named Gina who was dating Manuel. Once she realized that I was just friends with the boys, she told the other girls and then we all started staying together. Gina and I became close and Danny started dating a girl who hated me. So it was hard for Danny. He would still come to Nanny's home every night, but it was different. Instead of us doing things together I was telling him about my day and he would tell me of his.

Children in the city grow up much faster than the children in the suburbs. To have sex at twelve-years-old was not a big deal. I never had a boyfriend, but I had crushes. I had kissed Sean that one day. Danny and the boys never did anything, nor did they talk about it. I was only thirteen-years-old. One night I asked Danny if he was having sex, he put his head down and nodded yes. I wasn't upset I was fascinated, and made him tell me in detail what he did to his girlfriend and what it felt like. He said everywhere inside of him felt like the 4th of July with fireworks going off. I realized everyone was having sex except me.

Gina had an older brother Charley whose girlfriend was not only sexually active, but very verbal about it. One time we were at the deli counter in front of the hot dogs and sausages. She began pointing out the various sizes of the boys we knew. I didn't even know they came in different sizes. Charley was a flirt and he would always say dirty things to me and make me blush. He would call me the virgin. I would call for Gina from the street up to her apartment, and Charley would stick his head out the window.

"Gina is in the bathroom, and she said to come up," he would say.

"When Gina sticks out her head I'll come up," I yelled back.

I knew Gina wasn't there and I was afraid of him. I was never allowed to sleep out, but this one night my Nanny gave me permission to sleep at Gina's. I was so excited until I got there. Charley was sitting on the couch, her mother was going out for the night, and he made a rude comment.

"Tonight, when everyone is sleeping, I am going to crawl in your bed and you won't be virgin tomorrow," he laughed.

When Gina walked into the living room, I told her that I couldn't stay. I never told her why, until years later. Through the years I would see Charley and he still teased me about that night.

My mother had entered my sister in the Miss Staten Island Teenager pageant and she won! Now the State Pageant was being held at Palisades Park. My mother was so excited that my sister was now Miss Staten Island Teenager. This made everything right in her life. Her daughter, with her beauty, was now fulfilling another dream for hers. I went with them that day and there was nothing for me to do. I just rode the roller coaster over and over again. I sat in every seat to see which was the scariest. It was a tie between the first seat and last. Later that evening, when the pageant started all our friends and family came. Danny and I had a great time, going on all the rides and eating everything in sight. We were built alike, and no matter what we ate, we never gained weight. Danny didn't come to see my sister in the pageant; he was there for me. That was the last time Danny and I hung out as children, and it was the last summer I ever spent with Danny and Nanny.

CHAPTER THREE

―――◆――――

HIGH SCHOOL

After moving to South Beach, Becky and I were together every day. My parents didn't approve of Becky because she looked and acted like a boy. Becky and I loved to sing, we had the worse voices in the world, but we didn't care. We would skip arm and arm together and sing "Tea for Two". We did stupid things, like we would go to the stores, stand next to the mannequins and pose like them and startle people. One year we stood outside the department store with the Salvation Army Santa. We sang Christmas carols for three hours. Santa thanked us as he had collected a lot of money. Becky and I talked all the time mostly about not fitting in with our own families.

The school year was beginning and I didn't know why, but the zoning changed for the school district. My sister went to another high school. I was looking forward to going to high school. I wouldn't have my sister spying on me. It was an all white school, and there could not have been more than ten African Americans, maybe twenty Hispanics. Boy, was this different. I had found Pleasantville.

But from the first moment I opened my mouth I knew I was different. Each new class you attended, you had to stand up and say your name. As soon as I said my name I would hear the girls cackling and giggling. I had picked up a sought of slang staying in Manhattan, a little of the Spanish dialect, and a little of the African American. On top of that I had a deep voice. The only friend I had was Becky, and we didn't even have lunch together. So the first few weeks were really lonely. Our school was great; we were allowed to smoke outside in the courtyard, and also at the front or back of the school.

I never went into the cafeteria to feel the rejection of no one wanting to sit next to me. Kids would grub cigarettes from me and I would get to talk with them. Becky and I would go to and from school together, we both complained about how much school sucked. Then one day I was in the library and about twelve guys sat across from me. A few of them were from my classes, one in particular I knew. He was a tall, big broad kid called Frankie and weighed about 200 lbs. He was sitting across from me with his hand tucked under his chin and just kept staring at me. I was reading, and one time I glanced over and he smiled. I looked up again and he was still staring.

"What are you looking at you fat bastard, you got a fucking problem with me?" I blurted.

The whole table of guys started laughing, and he stood up.

"Didn't I tell you she had the filthiest mouth? She looks so cute and adorable, but when she opens that mouth, nothing but filth spews out," he said laughing out loud. I looked at him.

"Go fuck yourself," I hissed back.

"Stop! I like you. I'm not making fun of you. I wanted the guys to meet you. I think you're really different and not like the other girls," he told me.

"I would hope not, I wouldn't want people to think I was a little pussy," I replied. As soon as I said that they all started laughing again. Then he introduced me to a lot of other Italians, and lastly to Matty. He was the only one who wasn't Italian.

I found my friends, Jimmy D. and Matty. Frankie liked me but I could never call him my friend – he was a lot of fun, he could have been a comedian, we were the odd couple. I remember one day Frankie and I were talking and the guys called out to him.

"Where's Ellie?" I would shift my body to the side of him and pop out my head.

"I'm here!" I'd laugh.

I became Frankie's girlfriend. Only after going to just one party with him, the following Monday all the girls at school who didn't talk to me before were now my friends. I wasn't stupid, they knew I was friendly with all the guys, and they were just using me to get closer to them. Becky hated Frankie and she used to call him "the fat fuck".

She would curse him and he would curse her back. Becky didn't want any part of the football team. She didn't like any of them. Becky was changing. Her parents owned a taxi service and she would work as a dispatcher there. She had her own set of guys that she liked. They were much older and I didn't like them. It didn't affect our friendship, she tried to be friends with the cheerleaders and boosters, but they weren't for her. She always felt like they were making fun of her. Maybe I was the only one who got her. If it were in today's world, everyone would think that we were lesbians, by the way we dressed, talked, and the bond we shared. People asked me years later if Becky and I were lesbians. I laughed and told them no, just good friends and that Becky liked the boys.

She and I were afraid of sex, by now we had seen pictures of what having sex looked like. Why would any one want to put their penis in an area where we pee and bleed from? How disgusting! Kissing we understood, but not that. She would tease me that Frankie would suffocate me if we had sex. They would probably find my crushed body underneath him.

PARTY TIME

I still kept in touch with my friend Gina. I had invited her to come to a football game. I picked her up at the ferry and as soon as we walked into my house my mother started in on me, right in front of her, all because I didn't clean the house before she came. We had fun that weekend, but she never came back. Who would after that and sadly, we eventually drifted apart.

My job was to wash the clothes for the whole family. Clean the bedrooms, change the sheets, clean the bathroom upstairs, and the basement where Mikie's bedroom was. When the chandelier and the china closet had to be cleaned that too was my job. Marion's job was to clean the kitchen, living and dining rooms, which my mother ended up doing every day. I was not allowed to leave on a Saturday until all my chores were done, which meant I very rarely went out. It never stopped me. I always found a way to get out and have fun.

One night I was invited to a party at one of the cheerleader's houses. The guys had planned their own party, and now the girls decided to do the same. Arriving at the party one girl asked me if I could buy some alcohol. She gave me money, so Caroline who looked older, came with me. We walked to the liquor store and found three guys hanging out. We gave them money to buy the alcohol. They offered us a ride and when they heard there was a bunch of girls having a party, they asked could they come in. I told them no, and then they tried to break into the house. The girls started screaming, but then we heard different voices and realized that *our boys* were outside beating these guys up. Everything was starting to calm down when Frankie walked in.

"Where is she? I know it was her." he screamed, and then shouted out my last name.

"Connelly! Where are you? I know you would be the only one to bring those guys here," he accused. "It has to be you," he was yelling.

"It was me," I called back, "and we had so much fun. Furthermore, it got you here didn't it?" I asked, giving him my smartass attitude.

"Do you know what they could have done to you? Are you stupid?" He looked at me. "You weren't afraid were you, all the other girls were screaming and you weren't one of them. Are you afraid of anything?" Frankie asked, shaking his head.

"Yes, sex with you," I laughed.

Everyone burst out laughing. That was the night my reputation started.

MY ATTRACTION

At Christmastime Frankie and I had a fight and we broke up. Becky and I went ice-skating with all the girls, back then hitchhiking was the thing to do. There were five of us and we got into a car with three boys. I sat on one boy's lap and because I had a cigarette in my mouth I asked where I could put it out. Being a smartass, he lifted his hand for me to put it out on, so I took my lit cigarette and went to do so, but just before it touched his hand he grabbed the cigarette and looked at me.

"I knew someone would do that one day, but not someone as pretty as you," he smirked.

All I heard was his saying that I was pretty. I was surprised when I found out that we went to the same school. Then Becky and I started asking him questions and having a conversation. He looked at us surprised.

"Can the two of you talk without cursing?"

"Were we cursing?" I asked.

"Yes, in a two minute conversation the two of you used the words, fuck, cocksucker, bitch, mother-fucker, bastard and cunt," he was shocked.

(Cunt was Becky's word)

"Don't you say bad words?" I responded. "What were you counting or something?"

"You are adorable, would you want to go out with me?" He looked at me and smiled. His name was Tony and we made plans to meet each other the morning we returned back from Christmas break. Becky liked him very much.

After Frankie and I had our fight, it didn't take long before I was seeing him again, but I forgot that I had made a date with Tony. I kept my promise, unbeknown to Frankie, and met him in the courtyard. I explained to him that I had gone back with my boyfriend. But unfortunately, Frankie and I eventually broke up for good. I don't think we dated more than a month. But, I still stayed friends with all the guys. I would hang out and pitch pennies with them. Of course I usually won.

SCHOOL DAYS

I learned at a very early age that boys do not respect girls who have sex with them on the first date. There were always two types of girls—the ones you fuck, and the ones you date. My friend Caroline had tremendous breasts. She dated all the boys, but didn't go all the way. She would only let them fondle her breasts. First it was one boy, and then every boy was trying to date her. She wanted to be any one's girlfriend. I liked her and sat down to explain that they were using her and really didn't like her. So, when the next boy asked her out, she refused telling him that I had told her everyone only wanted to touch her breasts. The guys were mad, they were yelling at me, and I yelled right back at them:

"Fuck you, she's a nice girl. A little stupid, but she's not a slut and you guys are not going to make her one. There are enough fucking sluts around this school to get yourselves laid. She's my friend and unless you really like her, you'd better not fuck with her."

They listened and respected what I said. They never bothered her again. My whole life my parents teased me about not having breasts. Now, knowing how boys are I was glad, because if I had big breasts they would never have been my friends.

I hated school, my mother put me in commercial courses and I couldn't type or do steno. I was great in my other classes, so I started cutting typing and steno. Then I realized if I did my homework, I was smart enough to pass the midterms and wouldn't have to sit in the class. I cut most of my classes. Once my parents found out they set new rules, no smoking, no boys, no cutting class, and no cars!

One day I was getting out of a car filled with guys, I had a cigarette hanging from my mouth and of course I was cutting class. I turned and saw my father standing there. I ran so fast up the school steps and he ran right after me. I ran into the office screaming,

"He's going to kill me! He's going to kill me!"

I jumped over the desk and ran into my vice principal's office still screaming. Mr. Pitman came out of his office and was trying to hold my father back, he couldn't. Then my father grabbed me and hit me hard, I fell across the desk to the other side. He screamed and cursed at me right in front of everyone. Of course, when I arrived home my mother proceeded to beat me up also.

My father never beat me, it was just one hard smack across the face, but my mother would use any object she could put her hands on, like a spoon or a shoe, it didn't matter. I don't remember it hurting. I would put my hands over my face. I didn't like getting hit in the face and I hated the screaming. One time my father was ranting and raving so I told him to beat me so this could be over.

This episode at school worked out well for me because now it was all over the school how horrible my parents were. The school really cared about me, unlike the other schools I had attended. In the past the teachers hit us, so what was the big deal if our parents hit us?

Becky would often hang out in the courtyard. She told me that Tony (the boy in the car that night we hitchhiked) hung out there. I would meet Becky after classes in the courtyard waiting for Tony to come out. He had never spoken to me again after I told him I was back with Frankie. He only stared at me. I would stare back not saying anything. When the bell rang we both went back inside, it was weird. We probably did this for about a month, then one day I was trying to walk away, acting really cool. Becky had a habit of dragging her dungaree jacket on the ground. I tripped and fell into Becky, when I looked back Tony was laughing hysterically at me. I never went back to the courtyard after that day.

Becky and I would always hang out on her front steps. Then one day someone arrived to pick up Dora, Becky's sister. We were shocked when we saw that the guy was my Tony! Dora had taken my Tony. She blatantly got in his car. Once the car turned the corner we raced to my house. We ran up the stairs to my parent's room and took out the binoculars to spy on them. Then it happened, we didn't know what they were doing, but there it was right in front of our eyes. Dora was giving Tony a blowjob. We thought putting a penis in our vagina was bad, but our mouth?

"I'm never doing that, your sister can have him! Ugh!" I said, disgustedly to Becky.

These were the days filled with such funny and vivid memories. Like the time when Chris asked me to go to the dance, his girlfriend had recently dumped him. He asked me to go with him as a friend. He was such a gentleman and came to my house, which was a distance from his. We had fun at the dance and I went home in a cab.

The following Monday, Chris sat with me on the stairs.

"Do you know why nobody will date you?" he asked.

"No, I don't, why?" I was bewildered.

"Well, after I put you in the cab the football team greeted me. Frankie told me that you were the only girl who ever liked him and I couldn't date you."

Chris didn't care and he was not afraid of Frankie. He wanted to date me, but I told him we were only friends.

One day a black girl was harassing this girl named Brenda. I went to the cafeteria to stop her. She knew she couldn't beat me up, so she decided to come back the next day with her friends. It was all set for 4:00 p.m. at the football field. Becky, Allie, Rosie, Brenda (the cute little girl who never fought in her life) and I had arrived. Five of us all ready for battle, and then we looked over the field and saw at least twenty black girls walking towards us.

"We are going to get the shit kicked out us today girls," I told them, "Brenda, run and get out of here. The rest of you just be careful of the girls with the Afros because sometimes they keep razor blades in their hair," I warned.

My strategy was to walk out there by myself and see if I could talk them down. If I couldn't talk them down, we were in trouble. I started walking towards them.

"You better not run away on me, Allie!" I said, turning back to them.

As I walking I saw this girl with spots on her face. There could not be two girls with spots on their faces like that.

"Delia," I called out quickly.

"Ellie is that you? What the fuck girl, what the fuck are you doing here," she yelled.

"That mother-fucking bitch over there with you was tormenting my friend," I pointed to Brenda, "I told her to stop. It got out of hand and she said she would have her friends kick the shit out of me."

Delia started laughing and pulled the girl over towards me.

"Is this the girl you told me about?" she asked, but the girl just nodded yes.

"There is no way on this earth that this girl called you a black bastard," Delia said, "Were you lying to me girl?"

Before the girl could answer I spoke up.

"You bet your fucking ass I didn't say that! I may have called you a bastard, but I never said black. In fact I know what I called you, it was a fucking bastard!"

"That's right, because Ellie you never say a sentence without the word "fuck" that's your favorite word," she said to me.

Delia knew the girl was lying immediately.

"For lying to me and all us girls, I should let Ellie go to town on you and watch her beat you down," Delia threatened.

"I don't want to fight, I just want her to leave my friend alone," I answered and then just as soon as the words came out of my mouth I heard a familiar voice.

"Soul Sister!" It was Denise and Cha Cha. They came running over and made fun of my girls.

"What were you going to do with them?" she asked, pointing to Allie, Becky and Rosie.

"We were ready to get our asses kicked in," I said with a smile.

We started laughing and Delia asked if I had cigarette. I took one out and passed it around.

"Everything is fine, these are my friends from my old school," I yelled to my girls. We talked a little bit longer, at that time there was no hug good-bye; it was a low five with a slide.

"Check you out later sister," I said. I told her that I would go back to the old neighborhood, but I never did.

Becky was so relieved; Allie and Rosie looked a little disappointed because they liked to fight. Brenda didn't run away, but afterwards she asked me a weird question.

"You smoked from the same cigarette as them?" At that moment Allie knew I was going to beat the shit out of her. She told Brenda to walk away right now and to get the fuck out of there. She knew I was pissed for protecting, what turned out to be, this prejudice bitch. Those were my friends and that was the first time I saw prejudice in kids. I thought only adults showed that. I did have many fights but I never started them, I was usually protecting one of my friends. I had a reputation because most girls in this school did not like to fight.

RUNNING AWAY

I hated my house, parents, and sister. I knew I had to get out. I wanted to run away before report cards came out. I would tell everyone at school that I was running away. This was a funny day. When I told my friends they had a going away party in front of the school for me.

People gave us money. It was Becky, Beverly and me. There we were standing at the curb, I stuck my thumb out and immediately a car pulled up, we hopped in and waved goodbye to all our friends. We got into a car with three guys who lived in Jersey. We were making our way to Florida. Beverly had an older cousin who lived in Florida; she offered us her place to stay with her. We planned on getting waitress jobs. What a dream. Our intentions were to have the guys drop us off in Jersey and then hitch all the way to Florida.

Well, it turned out that we became distracted. They were cute and going to a big party that night. They wanted us to come and offered to drive us to Philly in the morning. Now don't get the wrong idea, they were boys and we were all virgins. It was just a party, just to hang out. We drank at the party, but Becky was a bad drinker, she always got emotional. When the guys were getting gas we made phone calls to our guys back home.

I called Brian and told him that I loved him, and I was going to miss him. He begged me to come home, but the guy Becky liked worked in the taxi service and her call got traced. Within two minutes three police cars came into the gas station. The boys were taken in one car and girls in the other. I didn't want the boys to get into trouble, I told the police that I lied to them and told them we were all eighteen. They finally released the boys and we waited for our parents.

Beverly's parents came in. She hugged them and cried, they told her how much they loved her. Becky and I watched this through the window.

Even until today, I don't know why Beverly ran away with us. I thought she just wanted to be cool like us. Then my father walked in, things were a lot different.

"You are a piece of shit, nothing but a piece of shit! Everything you touch turns to shit. Get the fuck up. I know you don't even care. I see it in your face, you are not afraid or sorry, you are not like the other girl, and you couldn't care less!" he yelled at me.

I just stared at him not showing any emotion. He knew I hated him. Anywhere would be better than living with them and he knew that's how I felt. He looked over at Becky.

"The two of you are never going to see each other again. Now, get the fuck up and let's get out of here," my father bellowed.

I could see the policeman felt sorry for me. Becky was trying to conceal her laughter while they spoke to my father. I looked over at Becky and she was mouthing, "Everything you touch turns to shit," then she started tapping objects with her finger.

"Shit," she would say, touching the object. I held back from laughing because if my father saw me he would have beat me right there.

I don't even remember the car ride home with him. Of course, when I walked in the house my mother slapped me.

"You disgust me, just go upstairs and get out of my sight," was all she said.

The next day my father drove me to Nanny's house, I don't know why they thought this was punishment? I ran into Nanny's house and she hugged me. She wanted to know why I had run away. She reminded me how much she loved me and how it would hurt her if something happened to me. Then she explained all the bad things that could have happened and made me promise that I would not do that again. I remember my parents saying that I had run away three times, but I can only remember this one time.

When my father picked me up a week later from Nanny's we were driving home and he handed me a cigarette.

"Here, smoke in front of me. I know you are not going to stop smoking. Can we both try? I don't want anything like this to happen again, you may not see it, but I love you," he said, keeping his eyes on the road.

This was the first time my father ever told me he loved me.

"I hate all of you and feel like I don't fit in. I'm not Marion and never will be," I said, with a lump in my throat, "can you accept me for me?"

"I'll try," he said.

After that we became friends. He was the lesser of two evils to me.

When I returned back to school, I had to be good or I was being sent to boarding school. Becky and I would sneak into the bathroom to see each other because we were not allowed to be together after running away. One day a girl came in the bathroom to talk to me, it turned out that she was with the boy, Brian, whom I liked when I was away. The old Ellie would have beaten her up, but I couldn't. Becky was afraid that I would be sent away and immediately blurted out trying to protect me.

"Ellie doesn't care, she doesn't like Brian. She likes some one else," she said to the girl.

Then the girl turned to me and asked whom?

I don't know why, but I told her "Bear".

The girl wanted to know which one? Matty's nickname was little Bear, and his brother a year older was Big Bear. I knew I couldn't say Matty because he was my friend. I told her "Big Bear" thinking it would not mean anything. He was one year older than me. I didn't know him; I had just seen him a few times around school. By the third period Big Bear walked up to me.

"I heard you like me?" He smiled.

"Go fuck yourself!" I said. Who would have thought?

FAREWELL BAD GIRL

Big Bear was different than the other boys I knew. He was calm and caring and he also had a great sense of humor. He had the bluest eyes that sparkled. He asked me to call him Mark. We went to a steakhouse and had burgers. I never went on a date with Frankie we just hung out with everyone. He was so much more mature than me and Mark was a gentlemen.

The Booster's Club was about to have their tryouts and surprisingly someone asked me to try out. I did my best and had assumed that I didn't make it, then by the end of the day one of the girls found me and awarded me with a yellow carnation for making the booster team.

I was going to school and finally I had a real boyfriend. I remember my father saying that Mark must have been a pervert and liked little boys. It was his sick way of reassuring me that there had to be something wrong with him if he liked me, because I wasn't a woman and didn't have a woman's body. Matty stopped being my friend, he was angry that I was dating his brother. I met Mark's friends and they immediately became mine.

Mark calmed me down a lot and I liked going to his house. His mother was an alcoholic, which shocked me. I had never seen a woman drink before. Mark's home was dysfunctional, but I fell in love with all of them. They liked me and I helped them with cleaning, decorating, and playing games at night. They soon became my family. I would take his alcoholic mother over my mother any day. At least when Mark's mother was mean, she had the excuse of being drunk, my mother was just plain mean. His father was a quiet man with a great sense of humor who worked in Manhattan. Whenever I went over there they always had a big dinner. The evening would start off okay, but then Delores would drink and things would eventually end up horrible.

Mark knew that he could trust me and I would never tell anyone what was going on in his home. He never talked about his mom's drinking problem, because he had accepted it at a very early age. I was happy. I had Mark, Vanessa (Mark's younger sister), then Mitchell (Mark's younger brother) and Becky. It took Matty about a year to be my friend again. My parents didn't bother me that much because I was never there. I still cleaned the house and did the laundry every Saturday. When the washing machine broke, Mark would take me to the Laundromat every Saturday for over a year. Nanny came to our house on weekends. Nanny and Grandpa loved gardening, we only had a little backyard, but it was enough to plant a few vegetables.

Mark loved me. All we talked about was being married, we were fifteen and sixteen-years-old. Our first time together was in my basement. It just happened and I cried. I don't know why I cried, maybe it was because I was no longer a virgin, and felt dirty the way catholic girls are raised to feel. I remember going to Becky's the next day and telling her, she wanted to know everything.

I took Mark to Manhattan to meet Danny, they didn't like each other, neither one of them even tried. Danny was the first thing I gave up for Mark. Looking back I regret it because our friendship had been so special. I should have never let anyone come between us. My grandfather was diagnosed with cancer, and he only had six months to live. We never told Nanny that grandpa was dying, but we moved to Staten Island before my grandfather died. Mark and I were in love. He was wonderful, caring, and attentive.

On our first anniversary he had a dozen roses sent to my class. I felt like a queen, everyone told me how lucky I was to have someone who loved me so much.

When he got his first car he had our anniversary date on his license plate. We did everything together in the summer and we would take his sister and my brother to the beaches. We would go on day trips to visit his relatives that lived out of state. Whatever we did they were always included. We were always looking for a place to move to when we got older. We wanted to move away from our families. His uncle, who lived in upstate New York, showed us a house that we could buy when we were married. We were going to the Senior Prom together. But, the day of the prom Caroline's (my girlfriend) mother called to inform me that Mark's friend had just broken up with her. She was so upset. Caroline had bought her gown and was really looking forward to the Prom. I told her mother not to worry about it that I would fix it. I told her to tell Caroline to get ready. Then I had Mark drive me to Julio's house and I beat the shit out of him. I told him that he was going to her house and needed to apologize, and then he would be taking her to the prom.

He listened to me and we all went to prom. Afterwards the snake that he was, he came back to my house and wanted to cheat with me. My grandfather yelled at him to go home. I told Mark what he did the next day, and they were never friends again. The sin was that Caroline ended up marrying him. I felt that it was my fault entirely.

Mark graduated and my grandfather died that November. The night he died, Mark received a phone call from my mother; they told him to take me out of the house so they could tell my Nanny. Mark drove me around and finally told me that grandfather had passed. I lived with Nanny so she wouldn't be alone. Then my uncle moved in with us.

With Mark graduating and Becky dropping out of school, I was lonely. I was fine all through football season being with all the girls, but it was different. I didn't like school, and why was I even going to school? I wasn't going to need an education. I was going to marry Mark and have a family. Then everything changed, Mark started working and he was different, he made plans to go on spring break with his friends. I think it was a mutual decision to break up, I don't remember exactly what happened, but we agreed to have a date in six months from the date we broke up. We were too young, and I knew I felt that way. I truly never knew if Mark felt that way.

———————

CHAPTER FOUR

BREAKING AWAY

I n July, I got a job in Manhattan as a file clerk and I was living with Nanny. Becky was working in her father's car service as a dispatcher and we would go out on weekends.

I found new friends at the office and one girl in particular Mitzi. She was living with a man, unheard of back then. She was a rebel and loved life and sex. We had fun together. There were so many men who liked me during this time and I found it most confusing.

There was an attorney who would leave a rose on my desk every day. Then there was the guy whose family owned several newsstands in lower Manhattan, he would ask me out every day. They were sweet men but definitely not my type. I like to party and dance. It was Disco time and every club you went into you danced. This particular year I did get closer to my mother, my father was strict and didn't want me going out.

I had to be home by mid-night, which was hard because the clubs didn't open until 10:00 p.m. So she covered up for me a lot. My father made it hard for me to grow and see what type of person I could be. Almost everyday he would tell me to call Mark because no one was ever going to love me except Mark. So here I am eighteen being told that Mark was the only man that would ever love me. Mark and I kept our date to meet in August, we went on a day trip to Washington DC. We had fun, but it wasn't the same. We argued a lot, but also we laughed a lot too. We never set a date to meet again. I moved to Florida for a few months with my cousin. I didn't like it there and decided to return to my job in Manhattan.

The following September, the office I was working at was closing. We were allowed to take longer lunch hours if we were looking for a job. So Mitzi and I walked into an employment agency where I met Tim. He was a thirty-year-old man living in Manhattan in an apartment on Seventieth Avenue. He liked me and asked to go out on a date that evening to dinner and a club. He planned on taking me back to the Ferry and I would get a cab on the Staten Island side. As we were walking to the Ferry I heard the announcement that this was the last Ferry until 6:00 a.m. I said nothing I wasn't taking the ferry alone at that time at night. When we reached Staten Island, a man told Tim that this was the last Ferry (from Staten Island/New York City) until 6:00 a.m. He then said that he would have to go home with me.

I told him he couldn't that my father would kill him. He was thirty-years-old. So the poor guy took me home in a cab. Then he took the cab to his mother's in Brooklyn to get money, because he didn't take his wallet. He then took the subway back to his apartment in Manhattan.

When I walked into his office the next day I apologized to him, I told him the truth that I had heard the announcement, but I was not taking the Ferry alone. We laughed about it and he asked if we could go out again that evening. We went out, but I told him that I did not want to have a relationship and be tied down. He agreed because he had just ended a two-year relationship. We went to clubs and dinner, some nights we would hang out in his apartment, and he always sent me home in a taxi every night.

I never saw him on the weekends and he never tried anything, we had been dating about one month when he told me he was impotent. I never knew this could happen to a man, I didn't care I wasn't ready for sex with him yet and I liked him. Then one night we were in his apartment and suddenly he wasn't impotent. Well, you would have thought I was a fucking miracle worker.

Everything changed, now he wanted to be together on the weekends and every night. He called me one night to tell me that he loved me and we needed to be together. He wanted a serious relationship. I told him bluntly I did not want a relationship, I liked what we had, it was simple, no commitment. I could never bring home a thirty-year-old man. So, as fast as it started it ended just as fast. I had my first affair.

I liked the freedom of going out with my friends. There were three clubs I would go to. One was watching the fifties/sixties groups perform, another was a disco and the other was a neighborhood bar. I had different groups of friends for each. Becky and I would go to the fifties club. Beverly and I would go to the neighborhood bar, and Carla I would go to the disco's.

Becky's father was dying of cancer and Becky's mother had left the father a few months before he had been diagnosed. Becky worked full time in the car service and lived and cared for her father. Going out and drinking together was her way to release her stress.

CUTE TONY

One night Becky and I went out and we ran into Tony, who we hadn't seen in years. There was always a little flirtation between us. He knew I was with Mark so he never did anything, but he would always smile at us when he saw us together. Becky and I were sitting at our table and Tony came over.

"What no boyfriends?" he asked. Becky was already drunk.

"Nope my girlfriend Ellie here is single," she slurred. Tony gave me a devilish smile and sat down next to me.

"That's good to hear. Ellie, remember the car ride years ago?" he asked. "You are still the only person who has ever done that." He pointed his finger at me. "I watched the two of you for years and you are still crazy."

"We just like to have fun; you have a fucking problem with that?" Becky said.

"I was waiting for that, because you two can't talk without cursing." he said.

"We even have songs that we sing with curses in them. Do you want to hear some?" she was provoking him.

"No, Becky, you are not singing that song."

"Why, you're a lady now? You don't want Tony to hear our songs?"

"Yes, I don't want Tony to hear our songs," I told her getting annoyed.

"I really would like to hear them," Tony said.

"I'll just do the juvenile delinquent song," she said and sang it. Tony was laughing and wanted to know what the other song was. Becky began to sing the disgusting song. I would never repeat it today. I remember the song word for word listening to her sing it to Tony. Tony eyes popped out his head and he was shocked.

"Is this what the two of you do?"

Becky began singing the verse again and I started singing with her, he just looked at me shaking his head.

"The two of you are insane," and he walked away.

I was laughing with Becky thinking that we had scared him away but soon he came back. He stayed with us and watched the show and when it was time to leave he wanted to take me home. Becky was too drunk to drive and he offered to follow us. Becky would not let me drive and she drove home fast and reckless. I was screaming at her to slow down, but she still didn't listen.

When I finally got into Tony's car he told me.

"I have waited four years to be alone with you, and tonight I thought I was going to watch you die."

I told him that I thought we were going to crash. He drove me to the beach where we sat in the car making out. He started to feel me up and I quickly removed his hand. I told him that we were not doing that. We talked, kissed, and laughed all night and we both fell asleep. In the morning he drove me home. He didn't ask me out on another date. He told me that he had a good time and smiled at me.

We often hung out at the same bars, and he would just stare at me. One night I was in the bar and a horrible man sitting next to me asked if I would like a drink, I refused, but then he placed his hand on the top of my thigh.

"Look honey, you only come here to get laid, so why are you going to be so picky," he said with a filthy smelling breath. I removed his hand from my thigh and my friend Gary, the bartender, saw my face. I got up and asked Beverly to take me home. I was afraid, no one had ever talked to me this way. Beverly took me home and then called me from the bar and said that Tony beat up the guy after I left – he had become my protector!

I would go to the bar after the Disco's and the same thing would happen, Tony would stare at me, and this went on for about two months. Then one night, I drank a lot and I walked over to him.

"What the fuck is your problem? What the fuck are you staring at?" He was shocked, and took my arm and started walking me to the door. He told me to calm down and to go outside with him. As soon as we got outside I pulled away from him.

"Why do you fucking stare at me and why did you beat that guy up? Do you think you're my fucking protector? I don't need anybody to protect me, what is this between us; you only fucking stare at me, why don't you just ask me out?" I yelled at him.

"You're a nice girl, a tough girl, but I don't want to be in a relationship with you. You are the type of girl who should have a boyfriend, then get married and have babies. I only want to fool around and I know that won't be possible with you."

"Well, maybe I just want to fool around too, did you ever think of that?" He walked over to me and cupped my face in his hand.

"You are too beautiful to just fool around with. I don't even know you, but I have watched you for years and there is something addicting about you, your eyes are like a cat and your laugh when I hear it makes me smile. I watch you dance and you turn me on."

"You say I'm crazy, you sound like the fucking crazy one. If you like someone you do something about it, you don't just stare at them." I looked at him. "Well, please stop staring at me? If you don't want to be with me, I don't need your protection, and don't tell me that I should be married. Maybe I want to be that girl who just has fun, but it won't be with you. I see this as your loss, not mine!" I glared at him for a few seconds and walked away.

I didn't go back to the bar for a few weeks and the next time I saw him I walked by making sure our eyes did not meet. The bartender Gary asked what happened between us.

"Nothing, nothing ever happens with Tony," I said it loud enough so he could hear me. I saw him put his face down and bite his lip. A few weeks later there was a shooting in the bar and Gary was killed. I never went back, it wouldn't be the same without Gary.

I'll always remember my eighteenth birthday with Gary. I was in the bar and when it turned midnight, I was now legal to drink. Gary brought out a cupcake with a candle, and he gave me a party hat then had everyone sing Happy Birthday to me. He gave me this enormous glass filled with my favorite drink, a screwdriver and made me chug it down, and I did. Everyone was cheering and we all got drunk. Gary drove me home that night. We were friends and he was so sweet to remember my birthday. He was so cute and good. I would always make him laugh especially when guys tried to pick me up. He told me I was different from all the other girls in the bar, they just wanted to get picked up but he could see that I came to dance and have fun.

CHAPTER FIVE

WEDDED BLISS

My sister was getting married in February and she asked Mark to be in the wedding party. My partying days were over and the night of my sister's wedding Mark and I were reunited. By the time that May came around, Mark and I were engaged and planned to get married the following August. I had started a new job in Manhattan and was able to still meet Mitzi for lunch. I also reconnected with Gina. I was planning my wedding with Mitzi, Becky, Beverly, and Gina in my bridal party. Becky's father was in the hospital and sadly he was in his final days. I went with Becky to see him. He was a tall man and resembled Dean Martin, but the disease had deteriorated him, he had become all skin and bones, his arms had to be tied to a board.

It was the most horrible thing I ever saw, but we did have a laugh. When we walked into the room, together we went over to him and he yelled at Becky.

"Why are the two of you together," he asked. Having dementia he thought we were fourteen. I bent over and kissed him.

"I will never leave Becky," I told him.

"You are just a little devil," he smiled at me and we all laughed.

He died the next day. I went to the funeral parlor with Becky to make the arrangements and pick out the casket. We were two nineteen-year-old girls facing reality and loss. At the funeral service her mother walked over to me.

"Look how cold my daughter Becky is, she can't even shed a tear!" she said to me, I was shocked. This was the first time I had ever yelled at an adult who wasn't family.

"How dare you say that about her, she was there every day until he died, she saw him suffering, she doesn't need to cry, she knows her father is out of pain," I told her, close to tears myself coupled with sadness and anger. "Where the hell were you, your other daughter and son? Becky was all he had in the end. So don't you ever say anything like that again," I told her. Her mother stared at me and she knew I was right. Becky overheard everything and when I looked over at her, she knew I would always have her back.

The Wedding Rehearsal Dinner, what a night! My girlfriends were very different from Mark's friends. They all hooked up together, so needless to say the wedding was a little tense when everyone showed up with their actual partners. My football buddies from high school were invited at the last minute, against Mark's wishes. At my wedding my football friends started a fight with the Brooklyn guys from another wedding downstairs. A brawl broke out and everyone was throwing punches on the stairs and in the lobby.

Well, it was a wedding that was talked about for years. I never changed into my going away outfit, and went to the hotel in my wedding gown. A few of our friends joined us. Once we arrived there was a little confusion about our room number and it ended up that there were too many people in our small room, so we moved the party downstairs to the bar.

It wasn't just our wedding we were celebrating it was also a goodbye party. Matty was leaving for school in California and Becky was moving to Florida to live with her mother. So we didn't have a wedding night, by the time we got to the room we both passed out, and I don't think we were alone. I slept in my gown that night and I left it at the front desk for someone to pick it up the next day.

We spent our honeymoon in San Francisco, Hawaii and Las Vegas. Mark was making every wish I ever had come true. I was still shy about my body and being naked in front of him, but Mark lovingly understood. In San Francisco, I decided it was time to wear my fancy lingerie. I went into the bathroom to put in my diaphragm, well it got stuck. Mark heard my cries, "No, No!" He was on the other side of door trying to get me to let him in to help me. There was no way he was going to be putting his hands up there to get it out. Finally, I had success and let's just say there was no birth control after that, ha!

Hawaii was beautiful, but I got sun poisoning the first day and couldn't go out in the sun. Our last stop was Las Vegas, Matty was meeting us there and we also hooked up with two of our friends from high school. Matty stayed in our room the last two evenings.

I didn't realize at the time, but I came home from my honeymoon without a tan. All we did for ten days was have sex numerous times a day. The first few months were fun, Mark was funny he would do the silliest things, like play hide and seek naked. One day he hid in the pantry and I could hear him yelling.

"Babe, babe the door is stuck!"

I thought he was kidding around, but the door really was stuck and I couldn't open it. I had to call the landlord to get him out. We were so embarrassed. Another night I was making my special pot brownies when his parents and their friend stopped by unexpectedly. We didn't say they couldn't eat them, so Mark and I just laughed as we watched all of them get stoned. My mother-in-law loved the brownies and wanted my recipe. It was a really funny time. We partied every weekend and Mark would always get drunk, one night he actually threw up in the bed. It was horrible.

By October I was pregnant. I remember cooking, frying onions and I started eating them, something I never did before. I looked at Mark.

"Could I be pregnant?" I asked.

"God forbid," was his response.

I was really shocked because all we talked about for years was having children. Back then you had to go to the doctor to get a pregnancy test. They called me with a positive response. I told Mark, he hugged me tight and told me how happy he was. To this day I really don't know if he was happy. I told my mother, she wasn't happy and insisted that I tell my father, she made me feel horrible, and also my father's response that he was going to count the months to be sure I wasn't pregnant before the wedding. Meaning if I got pregnant before my wedding I was a whore.

We went on a vacation to Canada to see Mark's family and we had a really good time. This would be the last of our trips visiting relatives. Everything changed quickly, we moved into middle income housing, because I would not be working. It wasn't thought of back then to work and no childcare was readily available. It hurt leaving my job and all my friends, but I was happy that I was going to be a mom.

That spring Mark joined a softball team, I got to the first game and all the guys on the team were from the old bar where I used to hang out. To my surprise Tony walked onto the field. By now I was seven months pregnant. He looked at me.

"I told you so," he said, pointing to my belly. I just smiled at him and we laughed. Two months later my cousin was getting married and Tony was at the reception. I was dancing having a great time but some friends were concerned thinking that the baby may come early. When I went over to talk to another cousin, Tony was sitting at the same table and his friend asked if he could feel the baby. As he rubbed my stomach he took Tony's hand telling him that he should feel this. Tony placed his hand on my stomach and looked at me and whispered.

"You're beautiful."

It was an awkward moment for me.

A week later my water broke, we went right in to see the doctor. After examining me he told my mother and Mark that the cord was wrapped around the baby's neck and he would have to do a C-section tomorrow. I was never told. I wasn't afraid, the next morning they prepped me for surgery and then wheeled me into the operating room. To my surprise there were about twelve people in the room.

"Why so many people?" I asked the doctor.

"The people on the left are for the baby, and the people on the right are here for you," he smiled. When they started cleaning the area and marking where they were going to cut me, I became concerned.

"Whoa, excuse me, I'm still awake," I called out.

"We have to wait, as we don't want the baby under anesthesia too long," he assured me.

"Please don't forget to put me to sleep before you cut, okay?" I said nervously.

"Don't worry you will be sleeping before you know it."

I remember looking at the clock, it was 2:22 p.m., and Joy was born at 2:26 p.m. I woke up back in my room, and it was visiting hours. I hadn't seen my baby, but everyone came in and told me how beautiful she was. Around 10:00 p.m. I was crying, I wanted to see my baby. Finally, the nurse brought her in, but she held onto the baby, as I couldn't touch her just yet. She was beautiful and we ended up calling her Joy.

The next day when I saw Mark, he had come in with his friends, and I told him that I was in pain.

"Don't tell me about pain, I have such a bad hangover," was his response. Then right by my bedside one friend passed out, apparently he had alcohol poisoning. The nurses came in and revived him. They quickly sent him down to the emergency room. I was very disappointed in Mark, as these assholes had drunk too much the night before.

NEW ARRIVAL

The day after we brought Joy home from the hospital, Mark and I had to go shopping. We had nothing for the baby; my mother had said it wouldn't be right to have a baby shower so close to my wedding. Anyway, we filled the car with all sorts of stuff, Mark was already complaining about getting everything into the house, but upon our arrival home I was thrilled to see Barbara, Kelly and Tina. They helped us up with all our packages and admired the way I decorated the apartment. We always hit it off and had been friends for years.

Three weeks later I attended my cousin's bridal shower, before I went home I called Mark and told him that if his friends and family didn't leave the house I was not coming home. Nobody likes partying more than me, but now we had a responsibility. Mark went on this three-week binge and it had to end. I explained that we had a baby and this could not continue.

We still entertained every weekend, I drank wine and I liked to smoke pot. At first when we would have friends over I tried not to change. Then one night I was drinking and smoking when Joy started crying. I remember walking into the room, everything was blurry and I could feel myself wobbling. I knew I could not do this ever again. I was a mother and I was not going to be like Mark's mother. So from that night on I never drank or smoked pot again when my children were home.

My marriage wasn't all that bad and we enjoyed each other. The only problem I saw in our relationship was the sex. Being a smartass, Mark began writing an S on the calendar when we had sex. Then when we had a fight, he would show me how long it had been. My doctor had written various notes through the years, to my husband saying that I could not have sex for two-three weeks. I was dumb and didn't know that this was not normal. It was the only time he would leave me alone.

Things turned for the worse when Mark became a fireman. I didn't want him to do that job. I didn't like being alone at night, but he didn't care. He took the job and I adjusted. I loved my husband and I was afraid that he could die in a fire. He took a detail in the Bronx, one of the busiest firehouses in the city. He was so proud of this. I think this is when I started pulling away from him. He didn't care if something happened to him and I would be left alone with our child. I would iron his uniform shirts and when

I was mad at him I would close every button, because I knew how annoying it was to undo them. Soon everything changed and he would go out more and drink more. I knew I would not see him on St. Patrick's Day. He joined the Emerald Society because I was Irish. I used to love St. Patrick's Day, but now I hated it.

He worked a lot in the beginning and it didn't bother me. I think it was because I had my girlfriends. Barbara's husband was also a fireman, so we would all get together at least three times a week after the kids went to sleep. When Mark was working then everyone would come to my house. When Barbara's husband worked, it would be her house. As time went by I wanted another child, we discussed it, but it didn't seem to happen. One day I wasn't feeling well and went to the doctor. Unbeknown to me, it turned out that I was already three months pregnant. I was so happy and again I think that Mark was also.

BIRTH OF OUR SECOND BABY

Those months flew by, I was scheduled for another C-section and my sister drove me to the hospital. I was supposed to get a spinal block and have a natural C-section. I was injected seven times before my doctor came in.

"What the hell is going on in here?" he asked.

"They are hurting me," I told him crying. "The other doctor said my spine is crooked and the needle won't go in."

Dr. Brown came over to me.

"I want you to wrap your arms around me, and squeeze me when the doctor starts to insert the needle," he said.

I did what I was told, and when the needle went in I screamed.

"My leg!" The pain was radiating throughout my leg.

"Enough, your going to sleep," said Dr. Brown.

I went to sleep and my baby girl was born. When I woke up in recovery Mark was there, he was most concerned.

"It's a girl," he told me. "Her name is Dawn and you are never doing this again!"

Later that day Matty was the first person to come to see me. The nurses had just brought Dawn into me. The hospital didn't know that he wasn't my husband. I wasn't allowed to hold her because I still had drugs in my system. Matty gently placed her on my chest. We both sat there in amazement as she stretched her head to look at me. She was only a couple of hours old.

"She knows her Mama," he said. It was a beautiful moment. Later that evening when Mark was with me they brought Dawn in and she stretched her neck.

"She looks like a chicken," Mark said. I hated him at that moment, how different it had been with Matty. I was in the hospital for a week and I insisted that there would be no drinking because he had to take care of Joy. I told him we would have everyone over on Friday night when I came home, but not before.

The family came over and as usual everyone got drunk. About 2:00 a.m. I didn't feel good, and my stomach was paining. When I looked down I saw my incision was bleeding. I tried to wake Mark but he was not responding. My stomach was still bleeding. I waited until 4:00 a.m. to call Barbara. She came immediately and yelled at Mark to wake up and take me to the hospital. When we got to the emergency room they told Mark that my incision was infected and they would have to reopen it. I can't even express the pain. Everyone, including Mark held me down; it needed to be opened right away to let out the infection fluids. Scissors began cutting into me. I wasn't even given an aspirin, and at one point Mark looked at me.

"Just calm down you're making a scene," he told me sharply.

"Making a scene? They are cutting me, am I fucking crazy? I can't even express the pain. I have a four-inch incision and I can feel every cut," I wailed.

When we got in the car he said to me

"I need a cigarette."

I didn't say anything, just looked at him and mumbled to myself, *he needs a cigarette for what, for watching me get ripped apart?*

We finally arrived home, and Mark went straight to bed and stayed there. I called my mother at 7:00 a.m. to tell her what happened and asked if she could watch Joy because I hadn't slept. My mother didn't come until 5:00 p.m. telling me that she couldn't get a ride.

Mark went to work that night and left me with Dawn and Joy. My incision was not closed and it needed to be cleaned. My stomach was open and I could even see the membranes. I poured sterilized water and benadine solution over it and bandaged myself up. Barbara offered to help me, but once again, I was too embarrassed to have anyone see me naked. Barbara stood outside the bathroom door and listened to me cry as I cleaned my wound. It was horrible, I don't know if it was the way it looked or the pain that it caused.

When I went to the doctor on Monday he was furious that they did this to me. He butterflied my incision together.

"The man who did this to you should give birth to a baby through his penis," he said angrily.

"It was a woman," was my response.

"That's even worse," he said shaking his head. Looking back I probably had a law suit, but who knew. Mark never took any vacation time to help me.

———

In June my brother-in-law, Matty was diagnosed with cancer. He had a lump on his neck. I fought with him every day to have it removed and I promised that I would be with him for his surgery. I went with Mark's father to the hospital and I heard Matty screaming.

"I am not having the operation and I'm not signing that," I heard walking in.

"What the hell is going on?" I asked.

"Elle, they want me sign this. Giving them permission to take my shoulder if they feel the cancer has spread," Matty said crying.

"What, your shoulder?" I repeated. I couldn't believe it.

Then the doctor explained that if the cancer was in the lymph nodes, they would have to remove the shoulder or the cancer would spread and he would die.

"Then he's going to die, because you are not taking his shoulder and he is not signing anything that says you are allowed to take his shoulder," I insisted. "Just take out the fucking lump and nothing else," I told them.

The doctor said the only thing they could do was to leave it open and place the tissues in a bag to keep then isolated.

"Fine then that's what you do," I looked at Matty and he was relieved.

Matty had his surgery. When he went home my mother-in-law was always drunk and he had nowhere to go. He came to my home, and Mark went to work and left us. His wound had to be cleaned three times a day, just as mine had to be cleaned two months earlier.

Matty was tall so I had to stand on the toilet to reach his neck. I was sure I could do this because I did it for myself, but this was different. As I opened the bandage there was a big hole and inside the bag was human tissue and membranes, it was disgusting.

"Oh God, Matty, I think I'm going to throw up."

"Elle don't do it, I'll do it."

"No, you don't need to see this, i-it is really bad," I told him. I began gagging as I took my fingers to move stuff around trying to clean it.

"Oh my God, Oh my God I can do this," I chanted.

Then my fear turned into laughter and suddenly we were laughing.

"This is so disgusting," I giggled.

Three times a day this had to be done. I did not want Matty to see it and I wasn't leaving him alone. We bonded during that time and it would be for life. He stayed about three weeks and helped me with the girls. He was so cute after the girls were asleep he would tell me to go upstairs and be with my friends. I guess after Matty left I saw how alone I was and that led me into a deep depression.

———————————

CHAPTER SIX

REVELATIONS

When my daughter, Dawn, was only twelve-weeks-old, I decided to go to therapy because I was not doing so well. I guess looking back now it must have been post-partum depression, which I did not have with Joy. My sister-in-law Vanessa had convinced me to talk with her therapist. It turned out that we were a good fit.

I could express myself to her and I was able to get out all the negative feelings inside of me. I also shared the moments that made me happy. People assumed that I was having a hard time being the mother of two children. But, through therapy, I understood they were not the cause of my unhappiness at that time, in fact they were the only sunlight in my life.

I found a love with them that I never knew. My daughters gave me a renewed strength. A love I never believed could exist. So through months of therapy we knew that I loved being a mom. This wasn't the problem, we began going through my childhood. What can one say? It's good to talk about the past, to get the emotional turmoil out, but you can never really change it. You simply learn to understand and accept what happened and try to move forward. I discovered that I was the problem and had lost myself along the way. I was deeply depressed, lonely, and in a marriage with no love. My therapist went very slowly with me; she asked a lot of questions and let me talk.

In one of our sessions she said, "Ellie you are only twenty-four years old and you have lived through so much. Don't you see the strength you have? You are a survivor. Do you remember in one of our past sessions, I asked what would you do if you found a dog bleeding, and after taking it to the vet he told you they would cut the dog without any anesthesia, what would you do?"

"Yes, I remember," I said with tears in my eyes.

"Your response was that you would take the dog and leave, right?"

"Yes, what is your point?" I asked.

"Ellie, I'm bringing up the dog because the day your husband held you down and let them cut you, he showed he was not there to protect you. When you called your mother and asked for her help she came, but hours too late. So the fear you faced that day was realizing you were alone, you had to take care of yourself, and your daughters."

"Yes, you're right," I began sobbing and she continued.

"You took care of Matty. You did not give them permission to take his shoulder. Then you took care of him because you didn't want him to suffer the way you did, or to feel alone. You're always protecting people. Ellie, you never protect yourself!"

"What do you suggest?" I asked, wiping away the tears with the tissues readily available in therapy sessions.

"What I would like you to do is the **Step Plan**. It's very simple, four little steps and here they are." She handed me the sheet of paper and I read:

Step 1 - The Journal

In your Daily Journal you are to write down your **best moment** of the day and **worst** moment. Then write how **you are feeling**, nothing more then that. Please just write it and put it away until tomorrow.

Step 2 - A Job

Try to earn a little money to show that you are in this marriage together. Be a contributing member of the family, that way you are not resorting back to a child, having to ask your parents for money.

Step 3 - Learn to Communicate

Communicate with others, be interested and people will find you interesting, not boring. You will begin to find that the person you were before you became a mother and wife.

She told me I would begin to see a girl that is full of life, funny, and interesting. Not the one who is trying to be something she's not. If a person can't like you, they certainly can't love you. Maybe if that girl he married comes back, he'll remember the girl he fell in love with. She told me I could still be a mother and a wife, and not lose the girl inside of myself – I was the only person who could take the little girl away from me.

THE LITTLE GIRL

Once I found her again, I never let that little girl inside of me go. It's funny now when I look back. I'm fifty-seven years old, and I still have that little girl. I had asked my therapist what were the other steps and she simply said, "They would come in time and we would take **one step at a time.**"

It was the summer time and we had planned a family vacation with another family. We rented cabins in upstate New York, a family resort where everything was geared around family. When we returned home, we got together with our friends sitting around the table showing the photos. My girlfriend Barbara brought something to my attention.

"Where's Mark in these pictures?" she asked.

"It looks like this is the vacation that Mark never really went on. I don't see him do you?" I observed.

That statement truly opened my eyes, because it was the first time another person saw what I was feeling about my marriage. That day I decided I had to take Step Two.

Mark would often be away for days and when he was home, I couldn't rely on him, he wasn't really there. This was really hard to do, especially when you're living in a two-bedroom apartment with two children. He was always busy doing something on his own. I remember writing years later when I was finally divorced from him that I was lonelier when I was married. Now I'm divorced and alone, I don't feel lonely. Funny how that works, right?

So I went out and got a real job. I ended up getting a job on weekends at a real estate office

I truly thought this would help my marriage by having the extra money. I could be around people and be with my daughters. It should have been great, but unfortunately it went another direction.

SIX MONTHS LATER – CROSSROADS BEGIN

Lydia was the manager of the real estate office. Her brother owned the company. I had worked in Manhattan prior to this, so business came easy for me. I worked on the weekend as the office secretary. I would answer the phone and relay the messages to all the agents. Actually I should say that I became Lydia's watchdog, because she was never there on the weekends. I was bored, so I started working on the referral program. I spoke with Lydia and she gave me the go ahead with the approval of the owner. I liked the job and I started this referral project in the office years before there were computers. I went a step further and became a licensed NY realtor. Everything looked great in my eyes and I felt that now I could contribute more to the family. I felt that one day we could finally buy a home for our family.

I made a lot of friends in the office, my first was Brian, an older man in his fifties, retired from a city job, he was the only full time realtor in our office, and every one else was part time. Lydia and he argued constantly. Brian had a partner named Ben who worked part time and assisted Brian with his deals. It didn't take long for me to realize that Brian could not fill out the paperwork. If his partner wasn't around he would give me the paper work and ask me to fill it out, always using the excuse that he didn't have his glasses. I knew they were always on the inside of his jacket.

But, I liked him, we talked on the weekends and he would always stay with me when I locked up the office. He reminded me of my grandfather, that's a big compliment from me, and his name was also Brian as was my grandfather's. He had a troubled life, not monetarily like most of us. He had been married with two sons, one was mentally handicapped and the other son died in an automobile accident. It was very sad, his wife had a nervous breakdown and then moved to Florida to be with her other son. The weather and the facilities were so much better for him. Brian had built a beautiful home and he showed me the pictures numerous times. When it came down to selling his home on Staten Island, his wife refused to have him join them in Florida.

I believe that he always felt as if his wife blamed him for the son's death, or there had been too much heartache in their marriage for it to work. I don't admire many men, but I did admire him. He supported and visited her and their son monthly, never filing for divorce; he took care of her until the day she died. Brian contributed a lot to me in achieving that much needed sense of myself.

THE MEN IN MY LIFE – MY TEACHERS
There were also two other men in my life at that time. Today, I realize how people come and go in our lives to help us along our journey, giving us the growth we need at that time.

Craig was a part time agent at the real estate, and a frustrated actor trying to break into the business. He was tall, handsome, a curly headed man with a great personality. We liked each other. My daughter Dawn was doing child modeling and had a role in a Soap Opera, so we had something in common. We would talk about the casting agencies and the calls he went on for commercials. He also did dinner theatre; it was a very interesting profession.

During that era we could sell real estate for a year and then take classes to get a license. Craig and I took the class together. I don't know which one of us was worse. I remember both of us wearing sunglasses and sleeping through the classes. Craig needed them from partying the night before, I needed them to sleep because I was exhausted. We did a study night at my apartment, the night before the test, because we had learned absolutely nothing in the class. We finally passed the test and became licensed real estate agents, and we were good friends for years. The experience with Craig I will always treasure. He also helped me grow into loving myself.

At this time Tom was hired and became Craig's partner. Tom was organized and responsible and Craig was not. Craig was loud and funny and Tom was reserved and respectful, they made the perfect team. When I first met Tom I didn't know if I liked him. He was always staring and never said very much to me. The first time I talked with him, I asked what his previous profession was, and he answered a mortician.

"OOH-OOH!" I said. I didn't think we would have anything in common, but subsequently we had.

BETRAYED

When you work as an agent on commission there is rivalry. You walk a very thin line and learn not to cross or you lose the friendship. I was happy to see my second family on the weekends. When I would open the office, the first thing I would look at was the Sales Board and see which agent was leading. Most of the time, it was Lydia's name. It would impress her to see her name there, but it's easy to be on the top of the board when you take all the good leads.

My job was to answer the phone and give the agents the leads on a rotational basis. I was always honest. I think that is why I formed a bond with all of them. I would hear stories and all the problems that went on during the week when I wasn't there. I was an employee and wasn't competing with them. I never showed any favoritism to anyone. I went by the book and everyone knew it. Slowly, I started liking myself. I would come up with ideas, and help the agents out with their clients. Lydia was most impressed with me in the beginning.

I remember that our main office would raise money for a charity and our office was the satellite office, which would usually participate in their events. So I decided that this office should raise money going out with buckets collecting money from cars at a major intersection near the office. Lydia refused, but every one of the agents showed up. The girls wore bunny ears and tails, and the guys had top hats. Even though they complained, and Tom complained the most, they all participated and we had so much fun and raised a lot of money. The owner was impressed that I had taken the initiative. After that everything changed with Lydia, she resented the staff liking me, and as the weeks rolled along it was very clear that I was doomed.

I remember going to a real estate party for the Board of Realtors. I don't know why, but they had Disney characters at the event and the person who was dressing as Minnie Mouse didn't show up. They asked me to wear the Minnie Mouse costume, and I did it. It was really funny, the owner was impressed, but clearly Lydia didn't like me doing that— strike two was against me.

In my mind everything was moving forward and I was happy. I have the love of my daughters, my job, and it had come time for the quarterly meeting. Lydia was reorganizing the office and would make an announcement at the meeting. She began giving out awards and in her speech she named Lorraine as the Referral Director. I was shocked, as originally Lydia was not going to hire her, even as the part time evening secretary. The full time secretary interviewed her, told Lydia that she wasn't qualified, which wasn't true.

I just happened to be filling in that evening when Lorraine came in for her second interview. I couldn't believe her resume. She was an AVP at her previous job in Manhattan, she typed a zillion works a minute, when she typed it looked like corn on the cob just rolling and going bing, bing, bing. She was amazing, the fastest I had ever seen. She had just had a baby and needed a job for her sanity. We instantly became friends. Now, imagine how I felt, not only did she get my promotion on a project that I had initiated, but no one bothered to tell me about it.

When Lydia announced Lorraine's name, I didn't know what to do, but worst of all I could feel the tears welling up inside of me. I looked over and saw Brian with the other guys in our family. I saw the anger and disgust on their faces and they were shaking their heads. They saw how hard I had worked on that program. They looked more shocked then me, but looking at their faces gave me the strength to hold back my tears and hold my head up with dignity. Lydia was a bitch, and she hurt me. When I looked over at her, she glared at me. I didn't blame Lorraine, she needed the job, and it was offered to her. She had no loyalty to me we just worked together. I wanted to quit and never go back, but I needed the job for my sanity and independence.

MY FIRST SALE

That night changed my life. The support I received from the guys was amazing. They all encouraged me to get into the sales side of the business, not the management side. They didn't want me to leave and wanted me to show Lydia that she wasn't going to push me out. So with the advice of my friends, I left my weekend position as secretary and became a weekend sales agent. I hired and trained my replacement, and her name was Sophia. Everything was working out fine. I was on rotation with all the other agents. Sophia had become one my friends during those months. She was a sweet woman, married with three children. Basically the same as me, she needed a job for a little extra money and sanity. Once again change was occurring and I was growing; now I was to learn the sales side of real estate.

Brian was a hard ruthless salesman. When I first started training to be an agent, I would get a listing and he would take me to the appointment to teach me how it was done. We would split it 50/50. I had a client that was looking for a particular home and it was a *For Sale By Owner*, which means when selling on their own they don't have to pay commission. Brian came with me, the listing was fine and they said if we could get the price, plus the commission added on, they would give us the listing.

We went back to my buyers, they loved the house, it was perfect and they were two great ladies. I got to experience Brian in action; he remained firm on the price including the commission. Brian wouldn't budge, the buyers finally agreed and the deal was signed. He didn't call me Ellie, he called me Eleanor, no one ever called me that, but I kind of liked it. I don't know why and I never asked him.

"Eleanor that is how it is done," he said.

"I love you Brian, but I can't do that," I looked at him.

"You will learn, he said smugly.

I just shook my head and he knew I could never do that.

We were both so excited. We were the listing agents and selling agents, which meant double commissions. Not so fast, Lydia informed us that we didn't get the listing. We were only entitled to get the sales commission, because the sellers did not sign a six-month contract (my second screw from Lydia). I went right over her head to the owner. I told him that he didn't have to pay any advertising expenses, he had no headaches selling the house, and so he overruled Lydia's decision and gave Brian and me the listing commission too. Lydia was out for blood. I walked out of the office and just glared at her. I helped Brian with his paperwork and he took me under his wing, he taught me the art of selling, which I rarely did after that.

THE UNIMAGINABLE

I made my first sale, but I wasn't comfortable going out on listings alone, so Tom offered to assist me. The very first listing I asked him to help me with went ever so smoothly. Tom basically did all the work, and all I did was get the appointment. I had my first six-month signed listing. We soon had appointments scheduled to show buyers the home. When I tried to reach the sellers, they were not answering. I called Tom to let him know that I was not getting any returned calls. The couple had appeared anxious to sell their home, and to me it didn't make any sense. Later that day, about 4:30 p.m., I got a call from Mr. Gonzales and his voice was shaking.

"Ellie, I have to take the house off the market, I have a problem. Could Tom and you come over with the release papers?" he asked, I couldn't refuse.

I called Tom immediately and we drove over to the home. We had no idea what we were walking into. Mr. Gonzales opened the door. He was in a panic, and not making any sense.

"Where's your wife?" I asked, repeating the question over and over. He finally got it out.

"S-she is upstairs . . . s-she tried to kill herself," he lamented.

Tom and I just looked at each other. Without a thought in my mind I just rushed up the stairs. When I reached the bedroom, I saw this woman passed out on the bed with a prescription of sleeping pills, empty bottle in her hand. I touched her at first and then put my two fingers on her throat pulse to see if she was breathing.

"Mrs. Gonzales, Mrs. Gonzales," I repeated over and over trying to get a response.

"Please don't be dead. Please don't be dead," I wailed in panic.

I didn't know what to do, then finally a moan came out her, I was so relieved, she wasn't dead. Yes!

"Mrs. Gonzales you have to wake up, you have to get up," I coaxed her. She started to move. I yelled to Mr. Gonzales to come and help me, and screamed down to Tom to call an ambulance. I was standing at the top of the stairs and Tom just looked at me in amazement. Mr. Gonzales assisted me getting her down the stairs.

I sat her in the breakfast nook and I began going through the cabinets trying to find coffee and talking loudly to keep her awake. *Why did she do this?* I thought.

The EMT unit finally arrived, they checked her vital signs and two of them got her onto a stretcher and hooked her up to an IV.

The officer began writing up a quick report, and he asked Tom and me if we were family members.

"N-no, we are just their real estate agents," Tom said a little bewildered. Then without warning, the words no sooner came out of his mouth and we both started laughing uncontrollably.

Mr. Gonzales went to the hospital with his wife and Tom and I drove back to the office. He told me that he thought she was going to fall down the stairs. He could see the headlines in the newspaper:

"REALTOR THROWS CLIENT DOWN STAIRS AFTER TAKING HOUSE OFF THE MARKET."

We laughed again with relief.

"By the way, where were you, while I was doing everything?" I asked.

"Outside waiting for the ambulance," He said, turning to me and smiled, then I punched him in the arm. He started singing, "My wife took sleeping pills! Who do I call? My realtors!" he was singing it to the Ghostbusters music. After that event we had a special bond, we talked and laughed all the time. But, we never talked about our personal lives.

THE OLD DAYS

Right out of the blue, when you least expect it, one day Tom came into the office and told me that he had gone out to dinner with Jimmy D. (an old friend from high school) I couldn't believe that he knew Jimmy, and that all the boys I hung out with in high school. Tom told me about the conversation.

"They were shocked when I told them that I worked with you," Tom began, "I told them that this couldn't be the same Ellie."

"What did they tell you about me?" I asked.

"Well, they told me stories of your high school days," Tom grinned mischievously.

"Oh, she was cute and sweet, but she was crazy," Jimmy had told Tom.

"You were the toughest girl he had ever met," he told me. Then went on with what I didn't want to hear.

"He said that you had the filthiest mouth he had ever heard, but the best girl ever to hang with," Tom said. He looked at me in amazement.

"I can't believe it Ellie, that you could have done the things they told me," he exclaimed wide eyed.

"Yeah Tom, I was once like that, or I should say I was that Ellie before marriage and children," I said truthfully.

He looked at me and didn't respond right away, he seemed confused with my answer. Then he said "I would like to see that Ellie sometime," he teased.

"You just may one day," I responded back and we laughed.

MY REAL ESTATE CAREER

Not one day went by when one of us didn't bring up the Gonzales. I went to work that weekend and I had three sales on the bulletin board, shared with my partners. We attended our mandatory monthly meeting. My name was at the top of the board and Lydia's remarks regarding my sales were insulting.

"It is important to note here that all Ellie's sales consisted of cheap homes with small commissions," She said to everyone, obviously to embarrass me.

"Well, I'm in the lead. I am the top listing agent for the month, and furthermore, I quit!" I responded. I had finally had it with this bitch.

Brian and the guys were heartbroken. They didn't want me to leave. The owner came to the office and wanted me to work in his office away from Lydia, but I refused. I couldn't be around such a disgusting person, who was a wife and a mother. To write about this woman would be a chapter in itself, but she does not deserve my time. Let's just say you get out of life what you put into it.

Tom had been talking about getting his own real estate office and he wanted me to work with him, but it didn't happen. I went to work at another real estate office right up the block from my home. I had the commission money coming to me, so I wasn't worried about a salary. Talk about insanity, this company was the worse place I had ever seen. I felt like I walked into the twilight zone. The décor, the people were morons, there were no work ethics, and training was non-existent, but I didn't care. I needed to be working, and Tom would call me weekly to give me updates on the progress of the office.

Everything seemed to be growing dark again. I was working with these morons, doing sales, but they weren't my work family, I missed Tom, Brian, Craig and Sophia. I missed laughing and having my friends around, then one day a very striking looking girl walked into the real estate office. I remember looking at her for the first time, and she oozed independence and confidence. I knew I was going to like her from the moment I looked at her.

One day the manager was trying to train her and I heard her say---

"I got it," she said.

He repeated what he had just said and once again Victoria replied.

"I got it!"

He continued to repeat it over again. I saw her take her hand and slap her forehead.

"Sir, for the third time, I got it. I fucking got it!" she glared.

I was sitting across from her and I burst out laughing, turning my head away from them. Victoria was like an impish child, you could see it in her eyes, and her demeanor.

She caught my eye.

What the fuck? She laughed out loud mouthing to me.

"Are you normal?" I just kept laughing. Then she wheeled her chair over to my desk, grabbed my arm and repeated.

"You are normal! Oh, thank God, somebody here is normal in this fucking twilight zone of an office!" she screamed.

I kept laughing and our friendship started at that moment. She had said exactly what I had been thinking. It's over thirty years now and we still bust out laughing when we see one another.

We soon became partners, I don't think we made one sale, but we made a lifetime friendship, which was well worth it. Finally Tom was going to open up his office. Tom's cousin, Jimmy, was very successful in the real estate market. Let's say he was an entrepreneur dabbling in various businesses. His partner was Richard and they were backing Tom's real estate adventure. They were supposed to be silent partners, but Tom had the managing control. I had one meeting with them before the office opened. I introduced Victoria to Tom and we were off and running. I was going to be the full-time day secretary and our sales team consisted of Tom, Victoria, Paul, and Craig.

I was never a good salesperson, but I could train people. I could talk to people but I wasn't a closer. I didn't like it. I liked the office atmosphere, the family environment. I didn't like being competitive. I would have made a lot more money if I would have stayed a sales agent, but money was never my motivation. You can't gain trust and loyalty from your family if you are competing against them.

Tom really should have been an architect. He had such a creative side to him when it came to designs and layouts. I liked decorating and I loved the organization process, probably two things that don't go together, but we were a team. I liked being part of a team and I couldn't wait to go to work. I realized during this time in my life that I was actually like two people living the same life. I looked at everything from an optimistic point of view from the business side, but my personal side was falling fast. If I didn't have my job I definitely would have fallen apart.

MY MARRIAGE BREAKS DOWN

Mark had taken a back seat to my career and it helped me get through these years. He was a NYC Fireman, a window installer, and a bartender. We lived in Federal housing paying at that time a mere $250 a month, utilities included. Let me just say that I never saw much of him, and after awhile I didn't care, we had a goal. We were going to buy a house, the life he promised so many years ago. I had lived in apartments my whole childhood. I had always dreamed of having my own bedroom and a backyard. Mark knew that was the one thing I always wanted. He grew up in a home and hated our apartment. I remember thinking it was the apartment that he didn't like, but I later realized it wasn't the apartment . . . it was me!

Come September, I was buying school clothes for my daughter Joy . . .

Mark did everything like the banking, paying the bills, the rent, the phone, and the car. He went food shopping and everyone saw this wonderful man doing everything for his family. What they didn't know was that I wasn't allowed to shop for food because I spent too much money and didn't use all the coupons.

I remember so vividly that it bothered him the way I would wash the dishes. I put the dish detergent on the sponge and would run it under the water before applying it to the dish. He would tell me that I was wasting the dish detergent and that he would wash the dishes. I wasn't stupid, and it wasn't something to fight about. I would just tell him to do it himself and walk away.

There were times when I was impish, I would wait until he was watching and purposely go over to the sink and squeeze that dish detergent onto the sponge and run the water. For me that brought out such enjoyment, it was the little girl that nobody liked, call it defiant, whatever. I couldn't pay the bills because I wasn't responsible. I couldn't have money because I would spend it! My job helped, I had my own money and if my girls wanted ice cream at least I had money to buy it for them. What the fuck!

Back to September - Buying school clothes . . .

I called Mark to tell him I was going shopping. Normally he put me on a budget, he gave me money and I would shop. I shopped for school, summer, Christmas, and Easter clothes. This year he told me to just go to the bank and take out the money I needed.

I was so excited. He told me where to find the bank book, finally I was an adult and he trusted me. I opened it up and saw $6,500 printed in bold numbers. It took me a minute, and then I realized the only money in this account was the money I made from my real estate commissions. I called him immediately.

"Where's the extra money from the windows and your bar tendering?" I insisted.

I was so naïve when I called him that day. I don't know what I thought; maybe he had a separate account for the house. Instead reality smacked me right in the face. His response that there was no other money shocked me.

"Mark, I thought we were saving to buy a house, where is all the money?" I questioned in tears.

"You are doing so great with your real estate, I figured that YOU can buy our house," he responded.

I just hung up the phone and the words echoed in my head. At times that still echoes in my head, it's strange the things you never forget. I still can't believe I didn't leave him that day, but it did help to truly see what kind of man I was married to.

I was still getting together with the girls. Tina was the funniest, carefree and very sexual. She would talk about various sexual positions, blowjobs, whip cream, and the three of us would look at her in amazement.

"Ellie, I don't understand why you don't like sex!" Tina said to me.

"I don't mind it the first time, but the third time it really hurts," I said.

All three looked at me.

"You mean the third time in a week?" Tina asked.

"No silly, in one night," I said shaking my head.

"No fucking way," Tina shouted.

"In one night!" Tina and Barbara yelled.

"I'm not lying, when I go home, as soon as I open the door, he will wake up and we'll have sex, three times," I laughed, "If you don't believe me, I will call when we are finished."

I went home and had sex with Mark. I rang Tina's phone as promised.

"Tomorrow night we are definitely talking," she said enthusiastically.

Mark was working, so the next night we got together in my apartment. I told them how I would be so raw afterwards, and how it hurt when I would urinate, and my insides were swollen. They told me that it was not normal. I also told them when I went to the doctor, how he would give me notes for Mark that I couldn't have sex for whatever period of time.

"You haven't told your therapist about this?" they asked

"I thought it was normal," I answered. We came from an era where sex was not talked about, and I thank God that these friends came into my life for so many reasons.

I do want to add here that two years later my girlfriend had met Mark in a bar and she overheard her girlfriend asking him a very personal question.

"Aren't you afraid when you go into a fire?" she said, seriously.

"I treat the fire the same way I treat sex, will I conquer the fire or will the fire conquer me," he answered, obnoxiously.

I told her you just described my sex life with my husband and we laughed.

HEARING MY TRUTH

I made an appointment with my therapist and told her about the sex. She couldn't understand why I had never told her before. I explained that I thought it was normal.

"Ellie, when you first came here you told me that you didn't like sex, and through the years I have been encouraging you to have sexual relations with your husband."

"Yes, I know that."

"I thought you had a problem not wanting sex and now you are telling me things are very different, sounds like he's the one who isn't satisfied, not you."

"I don't understand," I said, totally confused.

"You are not to blame, but you need to tell him that this cannot continue. If he can't feel satisfied after one time, then it's his problem not yours, he is abusing you Ellie," she suggested. I had never really thought of it that way.

I told her about the problem with the money at the bank.

"Who is taking care of you?" she surprisingly asked me.

"I don't know. I don't have to be taken care of," I responded.

"Who took care of you as a baby?"

"My mother and my grandmother (Nanny)."

"Why your grandmother and not your mother and father?" She asked.

"My father wasn't around too much and I was always at my grandmother's house." She just nodded again.

"As a teenager who took care of you?" She continued to make her point.

"Nobody," I admitted.

"Nobody is taking care of you today; the difference is in your childhood you knew you were alone with the exception of your grandparents. Three years ago you walked into this office. I saw a baby with two babies, and that day you were barely only taking care of yourself. You have the sole responsibility of caring for your children, right?"

"Yes, that's right!"

"In the three years that I have known you the only thing that Mark has done was financially support you. Ellie, you live in this dream world of remembering your husband as the boy he was, not the man he has become."

"Maybe . . ."

"He does not support you emotionally. The physical support is not there and now you finally see the financial support is not there either. You don't see your husband at all, all you see is the boy you dated, and yourself as that young irresponsible girl."

"Why are you saying all this, that's not true," I cried, but she continued.

"Your husband came here once, two years ago. After only one session with him I knew you needed me. You needed me to listen to you, in all your young years you never had anyone listen to you, maybe they listened, but they truly did not hear you," She raised her voice, I could hear the intensity.

"You were raised with conditional love. Parents are supposed to love their children unconditionally, no matter what. I don't know how or why your parents raised you like they did. It hurts me when I see such a beautiful young girl fighting so hard to have people love her. Your parents did not take care of you; instead they raised a woman full of complexes about being short, small breasted, with a pudgy nose, not as smart or as beautiful as your sister. Ellie, these are the complexes your family gave to you, when in fact . . ." she smiled sweetly at me, "You are beautiful!" She handed me a mirror.

"I want you to look at yourself and tell me what you see."

"I see Ellie."

"Now look in the mirror and see your beauty, look at your eyes so blue, they sparkle like the water, you have a smile that could brighten any room."

I began to feel embarrassed; no one had ever talked this way to me before.

"Do you feel ugly when your children look at you? No, you don't, because they love you. I want you to know that you are not only beautiful on the outside, but you are so beautiful inside. You have such a love for your children and people, but you have to stop loving people who don't love you back. Ellie, you were emotionally abused by your parents and now you are letting your husband do the same thing to you. He has made you believe that he is smarter than you, but he's not, and he makes you feel that way every time you open your mouth."

"Stop, stop, stop! I can't hear anymore," I reached for the tissues to blow my nose. I knew she was right and only wanted to help me, but it was hard to hear the truth.

She came over to me and placed her arm around my shoulder and sat with me while I calmed down. Finally, I said that I realized she was right. Then she talked about the first time we had met.

"Do you know, Ellie, three years ago you couldn't even speak? You amaze me how far you have come. You have your problems, but you don't dwell on them, you simply push them aside and always look forward, and you don't look back. This is something you have been doing since you were a young girl," she smiled knowingly.

"You are right, how do you know that?" I asked.

"It's the work I do. You choose to only remember the good and not bad. You are not a little girl, and you have to start growing up and start seeing the people around you for who they truly are. Stop making excuses for them," She looked at me questioningly.

"What should I do? How can you help?" I asked.

"You know what Step Four is. I know you do. You are not ready for it right now, but when you are I know you will be fine, and remember I will be here for you."

She never said what Step Four was, but I knew. I wasn't married to a man who loved me, or if he did, he did not know how to love me. I remember driving home from that session feeling broken. It's hard to admit that your parents never loved you as a child. I made excuses for them my whole life, but now I knew the difference because I was a mother and to me my girls are perfect.

They are different as night and day. That's what makes each one so special. I love my daughters and they are so beautiful, not just physically but their personalities are also. I used to love waking up and seeing them. I wish at that age I could have been a better mother to them. It was hard rushing around getting ready for school, babysitters, preparing dinners, and as I look back at those years I wasn't divorced. I was married to Mark, and he never took any responsibility.

D DAY HAD ARRIVED

My youngest daughter was sick and the babysitter could not watch her because she had two children of her own. Mark was going on a whitewater rafting trip for three days with his fireman buddies. I told him he could not go, I explained that I had no one to watch her, and I couldn't miss anymore work. He didn't care and said he was going.

At that moment I finally realized this wasn't his family, the firehouse was.

"You selfish fuck, if you walk out that door to go on your trip, you are never going to live here again," I finally said it.

Maybe he thought that I was bluffing having another one of my many outbursts, but he didn't care and he just left. I stayed home from work the next three days and emptied his closest, I had the locks changed and called his brother to pick up his stuff.

The night he left I slept for the first time in years.
I started writing a lot more.
I felt like something was changing inside me.
I needed to express myself.
I started writing poetry.

CHAPTER SEVEN

SELF RELIANCE

THE NEW OFFICE

Over the first three months the office grew fast, we all had our routine and usually Tom and I arrived at 9 a.m. He always brought something to eat like a donut, bagel, whatever, he never asked me what I wanted he would just surprise me each day. I enjoyed our talks every morning and we set goals together. I did the advertising and worked with the agents assisting them in keeping their deals together.

We came up with the name of the real estate company and later Tom came up with the logo. I hired Vanessa for the evening secretary position on weekdays and we hired another person for the weekends. Brian and Lorraine had left Lydia's office to come and work for us. Lorraine worked for a short time as the weekend secretary, but soon went into sales part time. At our Grand Opening party everyone met Tom's wife, Jenny. She never came to the office to help set it up. I felt that she was spoiled and conceited. What I didn't like about her was the way she put Tom down in front of everyone.

Around that time, the fad in jewelry was to have your name in diamonds. Jenny had a diamond-initialed ring with the letter J on it. Then across her chest, she wore a nameplate, and on her wrist a bracelet, both spelling out *Jenny*.

"Maybe she can't remember her name," Lorraine would joke, she didn't like her either, as they were both very different. One day after the office opened she stopped by and was looking around taking notice of everything; she spotted a cork board above my desk where I had pictures of my daughters in their dance costumes.

"Are those your nieces?" she asked, pointing to the pictures.

"No, they are my daughters," I responded. I showed her Joy and Dawn's pictures.

"They are beautiful, how long have you been married?"

"Six years," I responded.

"Oh, that's nice," she said and walked into Tom's office. I guess she felt safe knowing I was married and a mother.

Victoria liked her because she liked everyone and was always funny, it came natural to her, and everybody liked her as well. After the party we went to a bar where there was dancing. I loved to dance and I was a good dancer when I was with my friends. This was the first time I had been out in a long time. I was uncomfortable, I had never gone out with Victoria before and when I looked around everyone was drinking.

I wasn't a drinker and never needed alcohol to have fun. Being married to Mark I stopped drinking and I wasn't there to have fun. Victoria persuaded me to dance, but I wasn't my usual self. I couldn't get into the music or the song—I just wasn't into it. When we returned to the table, I guess Jenny (Tom's wife) had a little bit too much to drink talking really loud and acting obnoxious.

"She even dances like a wimp." I heard her say to Victoria. At that moment I realized she was talking about me.

"Oh, she's so perfect, Tom comes home every night saying, Ellie did this and Ellie is so terrific. I think that she is a little asswipe," she mocked me. I couldn't believe what a classless bitch she was. Tom also heard her and he couldn't look at me. I was most embarrassed and put my head down.

The old Ellie would have gone right up to her and punched her in her face, but this Ellie just sat there and took it. I liked my job and I wasn't an ass-wipe. Tom was my boss and I treated him with respect. Jenny was a secretary, and I know for a fact that she was treating her boss the same as me. From that moment I knew the woman was a complete idiot. I never wasted a moment thinking about her. Through the years I was cordial, but never looked to befriend her.

I remember when Mark and I were together we were planning to move into my sister's apartment of her two-family home. I found out that Tom and Jenny were going to build a house right on the corner near their home. When Jenny found out I was going to be living so close the deal was dead. Tom had been working with an architect on designs for the home, he would come into the office all excited to show me the plans, but as quickly as it started the deal soon died. I really didn't want to be living close to Tom either. He was my boss, why would I want to see him everyday, even on my days off?

Victoria and Lorraine joked about it constantly, telling me Jenny would become my best friend, and soon I would have my name in diamonds. I never did move because by the time the house was finished so was my marriage.

SINGLE LIFE WITH TWO KIDS

Six months later Tom called me into the office, the company was growing and I knew he was looking for an office manager. I was surprised by his offer.

"Ellie, I'm looking for an office manager, Jenny and I discussed the position and she recommended that I promote you. She pointed out that you are already doing everything the position calls for," he told me, but there was more, "we could hire a full time secretary and of course there will be a raise involved."

I was shocked about the promotion, but more about Jenny endorsing me.

"Yes," I responded, taking a deep breath, "I really need this as my husband and I are not together, and I need to buy a car," I explained. I saw the shock on Tom's face.

"When did this happen?" he asked.

"About six months ago," I responded.

I had told no one, except Victoria and Lorraine. I didn't want my personal life involved in my business life. I accepted the job with one condition, rather than he give me a large raise, I would take less, if he could lease me a car through the company. I really needed the car as I now worked one day on the weekend and some evenings. Tom worked Saturdays and I would work on Sundays. I was so excited and proud. I hired Catherine as the full time secretary and Sophia worked the weekends.

Tom and I went back to where we were two years ago, allowing me to be creative, listening to my ideas, and letting me implement them. Tom remembered me talking about giving the top sales agent a car for the month as an incentive program. The day we went down to get my car Tom leased two cars, one for me and one for the future top agent. After hiring a lot of new agents, I held special training meetings for the new agents, and weekly office meetings with all agents.

One night Victoria and I went out, I started talking to this handsome guy (I think at first he thought I was trying to pick him up) but no, I was recruiting him. It was all business with me and I loved it. I didn't think about Mark, the only hard part was getting someone to watch Dawn full time. She was only three when Mark left, he never watched her, but he would pick Dawn up after getting Joy from school. Before Dawn turned four, I met this woman, Danielle, whose daughter Casey was the same age, she began talking about a pre-school in September. During the conversations it came up that I was separated, she offered to watch Dawn for me, I felt that this was a gift from God.

She lived in the next building. Dawn and Casey grew to love each other. Danielle and I were called Kate and Allie (that was a television show in the eighties). She kept her own apartment, but we were like a couple. A few months after Danielle started watching my daughter, her husband left without giving her a dime for child support. We soon became one family. I worked and we both shopped for food, but she cooked before I came home from work so we could eat together. She also did homework with the girls and most of all she was a lot of fun. Before Danielle I was all over the place, I had one babysitter in the day for Dawn, and during the evenings, a teenager who lived upstairs would watch her.

As office manager I split up my days 10-4 or 6-9. I would pick up Dawn from the babysitter, and then Joy from school. I'd come home, cook them dinner, do homework and back to work, then home again for baths and bedtime. I was busy, but happy. The only stress I experienced was when I did not have anyone to watch my children. Tom didn't like it when I wasn't at work. I took off Thursdays, as it was easier to get things done. That was my day to stay home with Dawn, and we had time together one on one. What she wanted most of the time was to play with her dolls. We would sing and dance, she was adorable. Joy also had her friends come over on that day, so the apartment was always filled with children. All my friends wanted me to go out now that I was single, but I was happy staying home.

I was tired and enjoyed my time alone, which was not often. Mark rarely took the girls overnight. In the beginning he never took them. It was three months before my daughters realized that their father wasn't living at home and almost five months before I told my family. His family knew immediately because he had moved back home. He was a fireman and had a rotating schedule so on holidays and Sundays I would tell them that he was working. I didn't feel ready for my family to know.

MY FAMILY FINDS OUT

Word soon got out that Ellie was separated, and the rumors were flying. My sister told me that Mark was cheating on me. My father thought I chose my job over my husband. Lydia had told my uncle that I was having an affair with Tom. I still remember my Nanny asking me that question after she had heard. I didn't think

I could hate Lydia anymore than I did. She was the cheating bitch, not me. I divorced my husband because he did not love me and that was it! Then Mark jumped on the bandwagon telling people that I liked my boss. He never actually accused me of having an affair, but made the innuendoes to his friends.

Tom was my boss and a man who saw my worth. He was in love with his wife, every Christmas he would be like a little child, excited about the gifts he would be giving her. Yes, did I wish it were me? Of course, what woman wouldn't want to be loved that way? I loved the sweet side of Tom, but then there was a very deep, dark side to him. Sometimes he would put up a barrier with everyone, except with me. Even on his worst days, I would explain that he was not treating everyone nicely and to please stop and he did. That was one reason I liked him so much, he didn't just listen, he heard me.

Having so many people in the office, the real estate agents, the customers and the silent partners, everything changed and the partners were now no longer silent. Hiring Jimmy's sister-in-law as an agent was a big mistake. This was when the drama began. Everything that went wrong at the last office was now happening here. Maxine would get all the leads from Jimmy and Richard, she would brag about her deals. Victoria and the rest of the team worked hard, but Maxine was always the top sales person. Richard came into the office, often sticking his nose into everything. Richard and I did not like each other from the beginning. He was a male chauvinist pig and the biggest bull-shitter I had ever known. I saw right through him during that time, however Tom thought he was a great guy.

One time he told a female agent to get under the desk. I went crazy, I immediately went into Tom and complained, it was inappropriate for him to talk to women this way and he shouldn't be in this office. Jimmy was a rude, obnoxious, little man who strangely enough, we became very fond of one another. Jimmy was bipolar and was like a whirlwind. Some days he would dress up in army clothes, or cowboy outfits. He was a little boy doing what he wanted to. Then on the other hand, he had a limousine with an exotic black woman driver, so go figure?

JOE THE DOCTOR

We were having a shopping center being built across from our office, some of the people dropped in to say hello. That was when I met Joe. He had come into the office to see Richard about selling his condo on Staten Island. Joe was in a ten year relationship with a woman named Stella; they were always on again and off again. He was nice, but definitely not my type. He was a guido, (a term for an Italian man in Brooklyn) and wore a gold pinky ring, gold bracelets and the king of hearts on his neck chain, however he always smelled wonderful. The girls always joked that they could smell when Joe was in the office. He was a handsome man, twelve years older than me and very sexy. I avoided him at all costs. There was something about the way he sensually looked at me and sex frightened me. He would flirt with all the girls and Catherine had such a crush on him. He was a doctor and would come over to each of the girls and rub their necks, when he started walking towards me I quickly put a stop to that.

"That's far enough. My neck is fine, thank you," I would quickly say, and immediately walk away from him. I'll never forget the day he came in when I was on the phone.

"Fuck me," I said and hung up.

"When would you like that to be?" Joe responded, making me blush. I vowed never to use that expression when he was around again. Joe didn't live in his condo, so I asked if I could use his place to train the new agents. He agreed but took advantage of that. He would call and make embarrassing statements:

"I know you were at my house.

What were you doing there?

Did you try the bed?

Did you see how comfortable it is?

There's room for the two us."

He knew I was blushing through the phone, and everyone knew when Joe called because of the way I acted. He was a flirt and he was very much with someone. I was not going to waste my time, but I did enjoy being around him, he had a great sense of humor. He was also too old for me. Richard was his best friend, so I figured that he wasn't a good judge of character.

Finally his condo sold, now he was looking for a larger one to move into. He asked if I could be his agent. Well, before Tom had leased me the car, I had an accident with my old car and it was in the shop. Joe had to drive me around, but he became very pushy asking me very personal stuff.

"So, you are not married, or dating, and not having sex? What are you celibate?" he would ask rudely.

"Yes, and I like it this way," I responded.

"Don't you miss being kissed?"

"No."

"Don't you miss being touched?" he said, slowly and softly.

"Nope," I replied, "I don't like sex. It may be enjoyable to you, but I can live without it, believe me I'm not the girl you want," I told him curtly.

Any other man would have stopped talking at that moment, but not Joe. He had to know why over and over again. He could not break me. I was not going to open up to him. During that time I had very bad periods, probably from the stress I didn't even realize I was under. One day I became exasperated with him.

"Look I have blood clots coming out of me the size of golf balls. Okay? I really don't want to have a man's penis put up inside of me, do you understand?"

"The size of golf balls? Have you seen a doctor?" he asked.

I thought to myself: *He must be the stupidest man alive, there's nothing that turns him off.* Then one day I was showing him a condo, the owners were not home. When I went into the bedroom, he grabbed me and started kissing me. I pushed his hands off, and ran out of the house. I was standing by his car yelling at him as he walked down the stairs.

"Don't ever do that again, do you understand me?"

"I promise. I'll be a complete gentleman."

The next house we visited the homeowners were there. Going up the stairs he offered for me to go first.

"Thank you," I said.

"The view is so much better now," he crooned.

"You are just a pig!" I said, shaking my head.

He started laughing. I probably ended up showing Joe twenty houses. He didn't buy anything. Another day when I was out showing him houses, Tom had asked where I was and Catherine told him. When Joe dropped me off, Tom was standing, looking out the office window like a mad father.

"Where were you?" he asked.

"Showing, Dr. Joe a condo."

"You're the office manager, you are not an agent, and you don't show homes on my time," he was really mad.

"Maxine, I want you take Dr. Joe to look at houses."

"Yes, of course," Maxine smiled, looking over at me.

This incident started gossip in the office. Everyone thought that Tom was jealous. But, I didn't think so because I was the manager and should have been working in the office. After that I never let Tom see me with Joe. He called me constantly and Maxine would take him out to show him properties, but he didn't buy from her.

Joe became my friend. He called weekly, stopped in now and again, but never came over to my desk. He would peek his head around and wave his fingers. Of course I would always blush, and then he would give me that smile. He was wearing me down; he was a persistent little sucker.

One night I was out with my girlfriend Julia when I saw my husband Mark, he was with another woman. She was a firewoman—the biggest woman I had ever seen! I wasn't mad that he was with someone, I was mad because he knew I went to that bar. He acted like a dick, (I had always called him that) sending me a drink, kissing her in front of me.

"I can't believe you are so calm, Ellie," said Julia, "Why don't you beat the shit out of her?"

"You have to be kidding, she carried my weight on the fire exam," I replied.

I knew that this would not be a battle I could not win.

The next day Mark called and we argued about the woman he was with.

"She is more of a woman than you could ever be," he sneered. I was furious and knew that sex was my problem. Years of therapy, and still no answer, this was a sore subject for me.

That afternoon, Joe called. He usually called every Sunday when I was working. I was there alone.

"Hi honey how was your week?" he asked.

"Fine . . . " I replied, he heard it in my voice.

"Are you okay? Is there anything I can do to help you?" Joe asked.

"Yeah," I said, " . . . yeah, there is. You want to have sex with me, right?"

"Y-Yes, yes!" Joe stuttered in shock.

"Here is my address, the girls are with their father and I'll be there at 5:30 p.m."

"I'll be there, have a good day, see you then," he said, excitedly.

I hung up the phone and couldn't believe what I had just said. What the fuck! What do I have to lose? Nothing! He has someone, and I don't have to worry about having a relationship. I have to do this for myself, for once and for all, I have to know if the problem is with me. I rationalized that he was a kind man and I had known him for months. I felt I would be safe with an older man, how bad could it be? Then I realized that my apartment was a disaster. I called Julia, my girlfriend, and told her what I was doing. She met me at my place and within in ten minutes we had it looking good.

The doorbell rang and Julia was still in the apartment, we looked at each other and together said, "Whoa!"

"It's do or die, just go for it," Julia said. She had never met Joe and when I opened the door I introduced her.

"Good to meet you. A-Ah, I just came down to borrow some soap powder," she said, turning to leave and giving me the OK signal with her hand.

Standing in the foyer we didn't know what to do.

"So what now? Do I just take my clothes off right here? I'm at your service and your every wish is my command. I will be your sex slave and do whatever your heart desires," he said with so much confidence.

He sounded so funny, there was no romance with Joe, he came for one purpose only, and that was to get laid!

"I think I changed my mind you fucking idiot," I laughed, "I'd have to be out of my mind to have sex with you."

Then to my surprise he took hold of me and we kissed.

"I will be gentle, I promise," he whispered, sensually.

We went into the bedroom and I found that I actually enjoyed it. I felt safe with him.

"Do you want me to stay?" he asked.

"No, you have to go and I have to pick up the girls."

He kissed me goodbye.

"Your husband is crazy, you were wonderful," he said, and then left.

Julia came down as soon as he was gone. I think she was waiting at her window watching for him to leave.

"Well?" she asked, smiling.

"It was nice," I said, with a little smile.

"Nice? I didn't bust my ass cleaning your house for nice! I want to hear that it was amazing, and you had fifteen orgasms, not nice," she bubbled, and I started laughing.

"I don't know, Julia, it was . . . good, and it didn't hurt. He wasn't like Mark at all."

"Thank God, my girl is on her way," she hugged me.

After that night, Joe and I had a sexual thing going. It wasn't a relationship, we still talked every week and probably only saw each other about four times in six months. It was fine with me because I really didn't want anyone in my life.

CHAPTER EIGHT

———— ❦ ————

UNCOMMITTED

I was really busy these days. I took a job at a furniture store two nights a week and on Saturdays. I wanted to save money to take the girls to Disneyworld. A few months prior I had bumped into an old friend who was still friends with my first childhood sweetheart. His name was Sean, and he had moved to Long Island when we were in junior high school. He had become a model and was coming home for the holidays.

Jose called to tell me that Sean wanted to get together. We had grown up together, I remember that Sean was such a cute mischievous kid, with bright blue eyes that shined when he smiled. We met in a bar on Forest Avenue and his mother, brothers, and sister were with him, so it was more like a reunion. Sean kept staring over at me, and from time to time he still had that twinkle in his eyes and that beautiful smile for me. He was gorgeous, talk about a whirlwind affair. It was as though time had stood still, he wasn't a stranger he was my first love, and I was his. We had sex on our first date and many nights to follow. He came with Vanessa and me to Victoria's home, in Hunter Mountain, we went skiing or I should say he did. Vanessa and I were unsuccessful at skiing. We spent my birthday and the New Year together.

One day my father called and told me to come over immediately, he was screaming at me because one of cousin's friends has seen me out with Sean. I screamed back.

"I am separated from my husband and I can date people."

"Take your business off Staten Island," he told me hatefully.

"What, you think that I am a prostitute?" I screamed, "I'm separated and getting divorced. You know dad, my whole life all you did was tell me how bad sex was," I yelled at him. "Well, you know what? I don't have to be afraid of sex, it's people like you that I should be afraid of," I glared at him.

"I like sex and if you have a problem then that's too bad. I'm not a little girl and I am not a whore," I spoke confidently. "Please tell the family that I am not with Mark, so they don't see me as a woman cheating on her husband," I let him have it and he was dumbstruck. I stood up to him that day and he never said another word about whom I dated.

Joe still called me during this time and I actually told him about Sean. Joe had become my friend and when I told Sean about Joe he insisted that he was too old for me, and I agreed. We were happy together, but he was still a child, a beautiful and artistic person and a free spirit. Going whichever way the wind would take him. Sean was quiet, but so gentle. He was a loner and didn't talk much about his past. He was great with my daughters. Dawn and he had a few struggles, she was tough and he didn't always get her, but she was only four-years-old.

Joy and he meshed. She would just sit next to him and watch him sketch. They were a lot like. One day he was looking at my daughters and commented.

"They should have been mine," he said.

I didn't answer him and I felt bad for the years we were away from each other. One conversation he had talked about us having children, I found this strange because we never said we loved each other. It was just expected, the way it should have been. There's a Lionel Ritchie song called, "Say you - Say me". That's how I felt. Another day Sean talked about the song "Same Auld Lang Syne" and he felt that song was about us.

BEGINNING OF THE END

Sean and his brother built a beautiful wall unit in the girl's bedroom for me and that was the beginning of the end. He was there every night and if I gave my opinion of what I wanted in the unit, he disregarded whatever I suggested and did it his way. I started seeing that we weren't alike, I had responsibilities and he didn't. He never talked about what he was going to do with his future. He did talk about us being married and this frightened me. One night after I came home from work, I made dinner and suddenly he had changed.

"What's this?" he pointed to the rice.

His tone of voice really bothered me.

"You mean this?" I said, pointing to the rice. "This is shit I guess!" I picked up the plate and threw it against the backsplash in the kitchen.

"When I work all day and come home to cook a meal, I don't like being taken for granted," I explained through clenched teeth, "furthermore I didn't serve you shit, you didn't even taste it, you just looked at it . . . now please get out," I roared.

My girlfriend Lisa's apartment was on the same floor, later she told me that she and her mother had heard the fight.

"There goes another one, he didn't last long," her mother had commented.

Looking back, I think I reacted that way because I was afraid of losing myself and I did not want to be taken advantage of again. I was married, I did not like marriage, and for the first time in my life I was free to be myself. He was around too much and I saw that he was not the person for me, nor was I the person for him. We knew this was not going to last. It was over by March, I was taking my girls on our Disney vacation with my babysitter and I left Sean in the apartment to finish. I saw him only once after I got back and it was over.

A few weeks later I heard that song "Same Auld Lang Syne" come on the radio and the verse played, just for a moment I was back at school feeling the old, familiar pain. Now I understood the meaning of that song. Sean returned to modeling and I heard later that he had married a girl in England. I never regretted Sean coming back into my life and will always cherish the boy and admire the man he became. I hope that he found happiness.

Now my home life became an insane asylum. My girlfriend Tina had been abused by her boyfriend and had nowhere to live. While I was on vacation, she moved into my apartment with her two children, and her two cats. I already had a cat and a dog in an apartment where no pets were allowed. I don't even remember those months, it was chaos and after four months I told her she had to leave. My poor children, I regret all the craziness I brought into their lives. The one thing my daughters can never say is that they were bored or lonely.

THE BIG C

After Tina moved out everything seemed to calm down, but that summer I wasn't feeling well. I was always bleeding and constantly tired. The job was stressful, but I loved going to work even though I didn't feel good. Mark started coming around more helping me out with the girls. We were talking for the first time in a very long time. We didn't talk about getting back together, I was fixing up the apartment and he offered to build a wall in my living room. I was grateful and only had to pay for the supplies.

I started bleeding very heavy in June. By July I had bled for over forty days. I went to a doctor who cauterized me, but it did nothing. By August, I went to see a specialist in Manhattan who offered me no solutions. Then I went to a new doctor, he took blood work and prescribed a sonogram to be done the week before. Mark drove me to this appointment, but didn't come in with me. I went into see the doctor, and to my horror I received bad news—he had found cysts and a tumor in my uterus, and there was a 90% chance that it was cancer.

The doctor wanted to schedule a laparoscopy and a biopsy, and wanted it done as soon as possible. When you hear that word cancer, you hear death, nothing else. I left the office in shock and I could not believe what the doctor had reported. I didn't cry, but I do remember driving in the car with Mark.

"What did the doctor say?" he asked

"It might be cancer," I said, feeling numb.

"We should sue those other doctors who told you nothing was wrong!"

Hearing that, I looked at him in disbelief. He was the coldest person in the world. It turned out to be the best thing for me because I stopped feeling sorry for myself and my anger came out. When I am angry, I get the strength from deep inside to survive, just like when I was a child. I knew that day we were never getting back together. The proper response would have been anything other than what he said.

Now I begin losing it again, I don't want to know if I have cancer, how do I take care of my girls? If I die what will happen to them, how will they remember me? I told no one else, not my mother, sister, not a friend. I had to figure out what to do. Then one day there was an argument between the agents over a sale, normally I would handle these situations without a problem. But that day I lost it, Tom had overheard and he walked into the room.

"Ellie, come outside now." I walked outside and tried to explain.

"I know I was wrong," I began, "I should not have lost my temper."

Tom put his finger to my mouth for me to be quiet.

"Get into the car," he ordered. I suspected that he wanted me to calm down. I didn't know where we were driving too. Then he stopped the car.

"What is going on? This is not like you, and you haven't been yourself in days, what is wrong, Ellie?"

I just started crying.

"My doctor thinks I have cancer and I don't know what to do. I don't know what will happen to my daughters if I'm sick and I can't work," I blurted it all out.

"Calm down, Ellie," he said, holding me in his arms without saying anything for a long time. He let me sob and sob.

"Okay, let's break everything down," he suggested, "You don't know if it's cancer, so you have to do that first, alright?" he said, and I nodded my head. "If the tests come back that you have cancer, then you get the treatment and don't worry about the job, I'll take care of everything. So stop crying, alright?" He said with deep concern on his face.

That moment changed my life and I wasn't alone. I had a friend, a true friend who cared about me. When we went back to the office, he made me call the doctor and schedule the appointment for the surgery. Then he made me go home.

This was a crazy time for me. All I could think about were my daughters, who was going to raise them it I had cancer? I questioned in my mind if it could be Mark, my mother or my sister, but knew no way would I choose them. I thought long and hard and the only person I felt would give my children the love they needed was my girlfriend, Gina. She could at least tell my children nice things about their mother if I died.

They owned a beautiful home in Long Island, she was married to a terrific man and they could not have children. I called her to spend the day with them. She had no idea why I had come. We had wonderful day and I watched them doting on my daughters all day. Jay had taken them out for ice cream and when he came home he kept talking about was how cute Dawn was with the ice cream all over her nose.

I went home and wrote Gina a letter asking her if she would raise my daughters if something ever happened to me. It may sound strange, but I was so relieved when she called and told me that she and Jay would definitely be there for them.

While all this was going on, Stella had left Joe and moved to Florida. I told him about my surgery, but I didn't tell him that I might have cancer. We were friends, he offered to pick me up after my surgery and offered for me to recuperate in his condo with no strings attached.

My sister-in-law Vanessa dropped me off at the hospital. I went in alone, in the operating room my doctor came in and he wanted to know who to notify, and I told him nobody.

"If it's cancer, please give me the hysterectomy and take out everything." I stated.

"I could wait. Then you could make the decision to come back for the hysterectomy," he suggested.

"No if it's there just do it," I said, "when I wake up how will I know?" I asked, "I don't want to have to wait hours for you to come and tell me."

He could see that I was afraid and wanted to know instantly.

"If you have a big bandage, its cancer, a littler bandage means everything is good," he managed a little humor.

"Okay, then put me to sleep." I was ready.

He just smiled at me and held my hand as I went off sleep. I don't think he ever had a patient who was so alone. I knew he felt sorry for me.

"Thank you God," I whispered. I woke up and there was a small bandage.

The first person I called was Tom. When Cathy answered the phone she screamed out to Tom to pick up the phone.

"It's Ellie!"

"Well what is the verdict?" he asked.

"It's not cancer, it's not cancer," I cried.

You could hear the relief in his voice.

"I knew it, I knew it!" He kept saying, "Okay Ellie, you take care of yourself, and I'll talk with you tomorrow." He hung up.

I called Joe and he said he would be at the hospital bright and early to take me home. Then the funniest thing happened when the nurse came into my room.

"I have a strange request, the man in room 203 thinks he knows you and wants permission to come in," said the nurse, adding, "It sounds like a pick up line to me."

I was so sore, but I was intrigued to see who it was.

"Yes, you can let him visit me for a few minutes," I told the nurse. She left with a look of disapproval on her face.

When I saw who it was I was delighted. It was Gino who owned the pizza shop next to the office. They wheeled him into my room. He had just had a hernia operation.

After that when everyone came up to see me it was a party, but Tom didn't come, he sent me beautiful roses instead with a note simply stating:

I told you! Tom.

When I came back to office it was a party again, Gino came in from next door and started telling his story all about his surgery. How he would lie in pain, and there I was, two hours later, walking around like nothing had happened.

"That's our Ellie," said Tom, "I knew that everything was going to be okay!"

No sooner had Tom said that Cathy blurted out.

"Oh no! You were crazy that morning yelling at all of us, right up until Ellie called. Today is the first time I have seen you smile since she's been gone." She was the kind of person who didn't know when to keep her mouth shut.

Tom showed his embarrassment.

"You are crazy," he said to her, and then got up and walked into his office. I looked and smiled at him. He knew I was saying thank you for caring. By this time it was Victoria, Lorraine and Catherine that knew what was going on in my personal life with Joe. Tom had no idea that I stayed at Joe's house to recuperate.

CHAPTER NINE

DECEPTION - JOE

Joe picked me up from the hospital carrying my balloons and flowers, joking and thanking God that I was only in for one day or he would have had to rent a truck to get me home. He was kind and attentive. He would go to work, but always made sure that I had everything I needed.

Staying in his home that week let me see his gentle side. I could see having a life with him. He would bring home dinner and we would talk all night. We slept in the same bed holding one another, but we had no sex. We were like an old married couple. By the third day I was feeling better so I decided to cook dinner for us. He appreciated that and never took anything I did for granted. One afternoon the phone rang and I heard a lady's voice screaming.

"Who is this? Who is this?" I hung up and immediately called Joe. He told me that it must have been Stella.

"Don't worry about her," he said, "if she calls back tell her your Ellie, I don't care."

After hanging up with Joe the phone rang again, but I didn't pick it up. I stayed only one more day. I was feeling better and I wanted to be with the girls. After that Joe called me about three times a day and would make plans to get together for the weekends. He told me he was falling in love with me and wanted us to see more of each other. He wanted to meet my daughters and my family, and wanted to be in my life. I still wasn't sure about him. Stella had only moved to Florida a couple of months ago. I kept making excuses and didn't want to move too fast in the relationship.

The following week I went back to the doctor and he went over the results from the laparoscopy. He had found seven cysts in my right fallopian tube and eleven in the left, also a non-capsulated tumor in my uterus, and over one hundred polyps going up the rectum wall.

He diagnosed me with endometriosis. He said that I was too young to have a hysterectomy, especially since I was less than five feet, one inch tall. I would be prone to premature osteoporosis. He was explaining that I was young; I could meet someone and someday in the future have another child. But for now, he told me that the condition that I was currently in I would not be able conceive another child.

He wanted me to go on this new pill called Danocrine, very expensive at that time it was $100 a month, which I did not have, but I was still covered under Mark's insurance as we hadn't been divorced.

"There are a few side effects to the drugs, weight gain," he began. I was sitting on the couch across from his desk as he started listing them.

"Hair growth on your face, your voice will get deeper, you may lose the hair on your head, and lastly your bust size may decrease."

My mind was racing as he listed the side effects. I kept thinking to myself.

"Okay, weight gain no big deal, I'm too skinny anyway. Hair on my face, I can tweeze or wax, a deeper voice is a little scary given that I already have a deep voice. Hair thinning is not too good, I already have thin hair, but breast size decreasing bothers me, I'm barely an A cup, how much smaller could they get?

Just as he finished talking I burst out crying.

"How do you think I will ever meet somebody when I am fat, bald, bearded, talk like a man, and have no breasts?"

He got up from his chair and sat next to me on the couch and tried to clam me down.

"Ellie, it's only temporary, only nine months, we need to stop the bleeding and by stopping the bleeding it will stop the disease from growing," he explained. I agreed not knowing that I was taking male hormones. Let me tell you . . . they did change me, and for the next nine months, let's say *I changed a lot!*

One day Joe called to tell me that Stella was coming back, he told me that she had cancer and had no one to take care of her. She was going to get her treatment at Sloan Kettering in Manhattan. He said this was not going to come between us. He was just doing this for her as a friend. My heart broke, and I knew it was going to change everything.

I told him not to worry about it and to do what he had to. He wanted to see me to explain, but I spoke truthfully.

"Look, you were there when I needed you, now she needs you, I'm fine."

This was in October and I was going through my own crisis with Mark. I went to get my prescription filled and I was told that I was no longer covered under his insurance. I couldn't believe it and had to wait until the next day to speak with someone. When I spoke (or rather cried) to the fireman from the Health division he asked me if I was divorced.

I explained that we were separated and he wanted to know if it was legal and were the papers filed with the courts? I told him the papers were not filed, he told me to rip them up. He suggested that I write a letter stating that we were living apart, and not legally separated. He said that I would be reimbursed once the letter was received.

"It was your husband who called this office to have you removed from his coverage," he said, "I think you should be aware of that," he told me. I truly can't recall how many times Mark's meanness would shock me, but this was really low. I had to borrow money from my family to get my first prescription.

I remembered my prescription card was going to be mailed to Mark next month, but when I asked him he said he hadn't received it. I called, and yes it had been mailed, they assured me that he did receive the new cards, because a prescription had just been filled.

The next day, totally unplanned, he came to pick up the girls, but I was already in my car ready to go to work. He stood right in front of my car and put his hand on the hood.

"I need to talk with you!"

Right at that moment my foot stepped on the gas pedal, just enough to move the car into his body.

"Calm down! Don't do it Ellie! Ellie stop!" he yelled, scared as shit.

I wedged his fat thighs between the two cars and rolled down the window.

"Do you have my prescription card?" I roared.

My girlfriend Danielle had just walked out of the building to walk her dog. She saw the whole thing and was in hysterics. Mark reached into his pocket and I got out the car, walked over to him (legs still jammed between the cars) and took the card.

"Don't ever fuck with me again," I warned him.

I got into my car and pulled back slowly and just left. I was still speaking with Joe every day. He enjoyed that story the most, and would joke with me saying that maybe it was better he wasn't around. He kept insisting that we would spend my 30th birthday together. I told him there was no need, but he kept saying that nothing was going on between him and Stella, he only took her for treatment and she knew about me and understood. One day the phone rang in the office.

"Ellie, its Stella," said Catherine.

Victoria, Lorraine and Catherine ran to desk to listen. I picked up the phone.

"Can I help you," I said casually.

"Ellie this is Stella."

"Yes, I know who you are."

"I just wanted to clear the air with you regarding my situation with Joe. I think it would be good idea if we met for lunch," she suggested.

"No. I don't think so. There is nothing for us to talk about. Joe is my friend and I don't think what we had was a relationship. I see no reason to meet with you. You and Joe have a history and I am not part of that," I genuinely believed that.

"You don't know . . ." she started, but I didn't even let her finish the sentence.

"I don't want to know, goodbye Stella," I said and promptly hung up the phone.

Victoria insisted that I should have met with her. But, what good would it do? It wasn't about to change anything. Instead I called Joe and was rather surprised with what he said.

"She wanted to confirm that here was nothing between the two of us, and as soon as her treatment was over she was going back to Florida."

THE MANHATTAN DEALS

The next few months we spoke about the deal in Manhattan, Joe had brought a referral in from a patient who was a New York broker. Bobby (the agent I recruited at the bar) had found commercial buyers for the property. It was one of the most expensive sales for our office $1.6 million. This deal had all of us so excited. The day of the contract signing we drove in Jimmy's limousine into Manhattan. It was Tom, Bobby, Armani (the buyer and his partner), and myself. Now we were in the big time.

I had never been in a real estate office in Manhattan, and the place was massive. When we went into Mr. Wallace's office (the seller) Tom and I went to sit down at the table

"You're the realtors, you don't sit at the table," Mr. Wallace said, pointing to two chairs by the window.

"That's where you sit!" he said, rudely.

Tom and I sat in our chairs as directed. Mr. Wallace was not nice at all, the attorney for the buyer was speaking, and trying to lay out the terms of the contract and then all of sudden Mr. Wallace stood up and shouted.

"Get out, get out all of you." He looked at the attorney. "When you screw someone, you should remember their face. Don't you remember you sold me this property two years ago knowing that it was going to be down zoned? Get the fuck out of my office now! Get out," he screamed.

We all left, we didn't know what to do, and it had appeared our big deal was gone. We were at the elevator and Tom was talking with the buyer, his attorney had left pissed off. I looked at the buyer.

"Would you do the deal without your attorney? I mean would you have another attorney represent you?" I asked.

"Yes, I would." he said.

"Okay then," I said "I'll be right back."

I ran back to Mr. Wallace's office. He was speaking to an agent regarding some island that was for sale. Then he looked up and saw me.

"Are you stupid, didn't you hear me?" he bellowed.

"Wait, just give me a minute, you have a problem with the attorney, the attorney is not buying the property, our buyers are and they are willing to get another attorney to represent them," I spoke confidently. "We are all here. I can have them come back in and we can negotiate the terms and then have a new attorney review them. What do you think?" I asked eagerly.

"My, you are a spunky one, are they still here?" he asked.

"Yes," I nodded

"Alright, bring them back in," he said, with a faint smile.

I ran back down hall to get everyone and we all went into Mr. Wallace's office. I went to go to my seat by the window.

"Where are you going?" Mr. Wallace asked.

"Going to sit in my chair by the window," I said, sarcastically.

"Oh no! You are sitting right here beside me at this table," he said pulling out the chair. "You are the only one of this bunch with a pair of balls and a brain."

I smiled, and got up and sat next to Mr. Wallace as they negotiated the terms. I was ecstatic the whole ride home in the limo. I received praise from everyone and Tom was so proud of me. I called Joe to tell him that the deal was going through and basically that's all we spoke about for the next month.

Joe was going to receive $10,000 from the broker. He kept saying how he was going to buy me something special, and that I would love it. We would talk about everything and he would tell me how beautiful my birthday was going to be. I didn't miss him because he was there for me. I truly believed that we were going to spend my birthday together.

We were planning our annual Christmas party. Tom and I loved Christmas and we would talk about the presents we were buying people. I would tell him what the girls were asking for that year. The first year at the office we went to the store and bought the tree together and the decorations, that year we had the party in the office. Tom catered the food and I made my vegetable Christmas tree, which he loved.

"You always put your personal touch on everything you do," he said. I will always remember that.

That year I picked up the food as usual. As Tom was opening up the food tins I heard him yelling to me.

"Ellie, how fast were you driving?" he asked,

"Really fast," I responded.

"I can see that," he commented, holding the tin of food that had moved all to one side. He started laughing and shaking his head.

This was our tradition every Christmas. Tom would go and get all the Christmas items out of storage, set up the tree, put on the lights and then he would look at me.

"It's your turn to decorate," he would say.

Everyone in the office was involved in decorating, and they were truly our second family. Although everyone was there, Tom would still help me with the ornaments that I couldn't reach. This year we were having a big party across the street. Everyone was coming, and I think it was over one hundred people. We had a DJ, all kinds of liquor imaginable. Tom had gone overboard and all I had to do was get dressed and attend. I had this beautiful aquamarine cashmere sweater dress, which buttoned down the back.

I was very comfortable with my second family Victoria, Lorraine, Sophia, Brian, Mike, Bobby, Catherine, Cathy, Frannie and their spouses. That night I can truly say the old Ellie was back. I danced all night with everyone and drank a little. I saw Jenny (Tom's wife) glaring at me the entire evening, but I didn't care. I was with my friends having a blast. When I was doing one of my dance moves, Victoria came up behind me and whispered in my ear.

"The whole back of your dress is opened and your ass is sticking out."

Normally I would have been embarrassed, but that night I was having so much fun I just laughed and laughed. Victoria walked me off the dance floor backwards holding my dress until we reached the bathroom. I don't know if anybody saw what happened, but before I knew it Tom was outside the door calling my name.

"Ellie, Ellie come out here, I need to talk with you," he called. Apparently someone had told him about my dress and he was teasing me.

"See if anyone has any safety pins please?" I yelled to him. He couldn't find enough pins, but he came back with a needle and thread. Victoria always teased him about that because he was so meticulous.

"Do you carry a needle and thread around just in case you pop a button? What man carries a sewing kit?" She went on and on. Tom laughed at her jokes.

Victoria sewed me into my dress and returned to the party. It was a great night. I remember calling Joe and telling him how much fun he had missed out on.

When my thirtieth birthday came around, Julia, Lisa, Lorraine, Catherine, and Victoria all wanted to do something special for me. Joe hadn't called and they didn't think he was going to show up. I told them that I wanted to stay home so there could be no excuses if he called and I wasn't there. I wanted to stay home, drink a bottle of wine, put on my Barbra Streisand albums and cry my eyes out.

I needed to do this. Just as I suspected he never showed up and I ended up crying all night.

He finally called the next day, but I refused to take his call. I didn't want to hear one more lie or excuse. He kept calling but I simply ignored him. I was heartbroken. With Joe it seemed that I only ever got a glimpse of what life could be with him. I was depressed and Victoria was going to California, she persuaded me to go with her. I went for four days and we had a blast. I had never been on vacation with just the girls before. It made me feel like a teenager. We drove to Tijuana and ended up on stage dancing with a mariachi band. It was the first time in my life that I felt totally free. When I came home from vacation I made a new goal for myself—I would start going out more with the girls. I did that for a few weeks, but it was not for me. I didn't like the bar scene, and getting picked up by guys just wasn't my thing. I like to get to know a person before I date them.

———————————

February rolled around and no word from Joe for the last two months. Our big deal was closing today in Manhattan. Tom couldn't be there so I was on my own. Bobby and I took the limo by ourselves. The buyers were going to meet us in Mr. Wallace's office. When I walked into the conference room I saw Armani, there was another gentlemen at the table reviewing paperwork. He came over to and introduced himself.

"Hi, I'm Winston Mathers."
He had beautiful blue eyes and he put out his hand.
"So, you're the infamous Ellie. It's a pleasure to meet you."
The closing went smoothly, Mr. Wallace thanked me for coming. I called Tom and he told me to take them out to dinner. I quickly explained that I didn't have any money. He told us just to go to the restaurant and everything would be taken care of. I took Winston, Armani and Bobby out to the restaurant. We sat down at the table and very soon Richard Larsen came over to the table and

congratulated us. He then informed us that the bill had been taken care. I was so relieved.

Dinner had gone well. Winston was a really nice man. It turned out that he was in the middle of a divorce, but he was such a free spirit. He would think nothing of reaching over and tasting the food right off of my plate. He was a real estate developer and was most interesting. He talked about St. John's and about the property he owned there.

"You have to come to St. John's," he told me numerous times. For the first time in months I felt something like a spark inside of me, a light of sunshine. He liked me and I felt terrific, he walked me to the car and shook my hand, he was a gentleman. I was smiling all the way home. Not because of the deal, it was because of him! The next day I went to work so excited, this was largest commission our office had made at that time.

"Where have you been?" Catherine asked, as soon as she walked in. "I have been trying to call you all night," she began.

I started to tell her about the closing and told her the name of the restaurant I took them too.

"You went to what restaurant, did you see anyone there?" she asked.

"Yes, I saw Richard Larsen."

"Did you see Dr. Joe?"

"No, why?" I replied.

"Because, he was there last night. Richard was meeting him to celebrate his engagement to Stella." She went on to say that Joe took the ten thousand dollars from the deal to buy her the ring. All the happiness I felt the day before gushed right out of me.

Oh my God, and I was there in the same restaurant. Thank God, I was with Winston, Armani and Bobby. I guess I was so involved in our conversation; I had never looked around the room.

I was heartbroken. Once again Joe burned out my flame.

I recalled a song: *At this moment* by Billy Vera.

Basically the song kept repeating over and over.

"Because you just don't love me no more."

Wherever I went and that song was playing it had become a joke between all of us. Every morning I would walk into the office and it would start playing on the radio, if we went in the car, it played on the radio. Even one of my favorite TV shows, *Family Ties* had the song. The next day, everyone joked about that particular episode. If it wasn't for that song I think I probably would have gotten over Joe sooner. It was a hit song for over three months.

CHAPTER TEN

IMMORALITY

I spoke with Winston from time to time, but he was in such a mess with his divorce. The office was busy and there was a lot going on. The agents were working on many deals, and it kept me busy. In May, Joe called the office and Catherine answered, she told me that it was Joe. I don't know what tempted me to pick up the phone. His first words were:

"Don't hang up, I need to talk you, I have a lot of explaining to do," he sounded nervous.

"I would say so," I casually answered.

"Can I take you out to dinner . . . just to talk, Ellie?"

I agreed, but don't know why. There was something about this man that got to me. I wanted to look into his face and tell him off so badly. The night I was meeting Joe, Victoria, Julia, and Lisa were in my apartment arguing with me, not wanting me to go. I left anyway feeling a little like Barbra Streisand in *Funny Girl* when she sang the song, *Don't rain on my parade,* and the first line, *Don't tell me not to live.*

We had arranged to meet at a restaurant near my home. He looked his usual handsome self, and I could see a certain excitement in his face. I later learned that he didn't think I was going to show up. Approaching the table he went to kiss me, but I turned my head and sat down. I looked at him long, hard and cold.

"What do you have to say for yourself, and what other bullshit could you possibly tell me?" I spoke with a woman's scorn.

"I am sorry for everything, I was wrong, and Stella made a fool of me," he began, "she never had cancer it was all a lie to keep me from you," he explained.

Apparently, she had deceived him after that day I picked up the phone in his condo. When she called, he told her that I had just had surgery. I guess that's where she got the idea to say she was sick, because he was taking care of me.

"You did not take care of me. I slept in your home to recuperate. You are nothing but a dick!" I said, pissed off.

"No that's Mark's name, not mine," he teased.

He could always make me laugh with his stupidity. I told him I didn't want anything to do with him, and he made his choice months before. I reminded him also of my 30th birthday, all alone waiting for him.

"You didn't even call!" I wailed.

He told me that Stella had a serious health episode that night, which now he knows was bullshit, but at the time he really thought she was ill. Now she had moved back to Florida, with not to mention the ten thousand dollar ring.

"You got engaged, and I was there at the same restaurant the night of your engagement," I told him, reliving the hurt I felt.

"I know I saw you. As a matter of fact I watched you the whole night. I even watched that guy walk you to the car, but I knew you wouldn't go home with him, not my Ellie." He was sounding a little over-confident; it was time to kick the legs out from under him.

"Look Joe," I began, "I can't go through this again with you. I'm doing fine, thank you. You should know that the man you saw walking me to my car was one of the buyers of our big deal. Joe, we are dating. He's a very nice, honest man. Unlike you!" I added.

I wasn't dating Winston, but I had to keep Joe away from me. He wouldn't give up.

"Richard didn't tell me you were dating," he questioned, puzzled. "Ellie, let's go out on Wednesday night?" he insisted.

"No Joe, I have a date with Winston, you just don't get it do you?" I said, and quickly left the restaurant, knowing that Joe was not going to stop pursuing me. I knew that he would start coming into the office and eventually break me down.

The next day I told the girls in the office everything.

"What are you going to do?" Victoria asked.

"I have to ask Winston out for Wednesday night." I told them, and proceeded to call him and put it out there.

"What did you say?" Victoria asked.

"I reminded him that we had been dancing around this for months. I asked if he liked me, and could we go out Wednesday night?"

This was how that conversation went.

"Yes, Ellie, I do like you," he said, "I just thought you were not ready."

"I'm ready!" I lied.

I hung up the phone, took a deep breath.

"Thank you. Victoria, Lorraine, and Catherine," we all cheered.

"Most importantly," I said, "thank you Winston." I was so relieved.

———

My office meeting with the staff was scheduled for Wednesday night. Winston had planned to meet me there. I was in the middle of my meeting when Cathy walked into the room.

"Dr. Joe is here," she announced, knowing what was going on.

I knew it! I knew he would show up. Victoria and Lorraine were the only other people in the meeting aware of what was going on. I began speaking to the staff, and not five minutes later Cathy came in and reported.

"Winston is here. Winston is here," She announced excitedly. At this point I began laughing.

"Well, I guess our meeting is over, thank you everyone for coming. It seems that I have a few things to take care of. I'll see you all tomorrow, I do apologize." They smiled understandingly.

I walked out to find that Cathy had sat Winston at her desk, and Joe was sitting directly behind him in Tom's office. I became flustered and walked over to Winston.

"Hi! I want to change and then I'll be right with you," I smiled. Walking to the bathroom I looked over at Joe and politely gave him the finger. It could not have been more perfect. Winston had only seen me in business suits and dresses. He was a free sprit type of a guy who always wore comfortable clothes. When I walked out of the bathroom with tight jeans and my button down shirt, Winston could not hold back his excitement.

"Oh my God, you look terrific! You have such a great body," he complimented me. Normally, I would have blushed, but I was excited because Joe could hear every word.

"I'm ready, let's go," I smiled at Winston. Glancing into the office, I saw Joe with his head down shaking it from side to side.

Our first date was really nice. I don't know where we went, or what we ate. I liked him, but he wasn't Joe and he wasn't Mark. He liked me very much and I decided that night this would be a new start for me.

IT'S COMPLICATED - JOE

Not so fast. Joe came into the office every day after that.

"You're a persistent mother-fucker aren't you?" rudely I would say to him daily. He would walk over to my desk and start kidding around with me, making jokes about Winston saying it openly so everyone in the office could hear him.

"He's not her type. He doesn't make her laugh, like I do." He constantly repeated.

"You are a fucking moron! He may not make me laugh, but he doesn't hurt me, he doesn't get engaged to someone else when he's in a relationship with me," I defended Winston, "you have no scruples Joe."

"Not with you," was his reply.

Any one else would have been embarrassed and walked out the door, but not Joe. I truly don't remember how he did it, but he did and he broke me.

So now for the first time in my life I was seeing two men. I didn't lie, I explained the situation to Winston and he understood. Joe thought I was cheating on Winston so this of course made him happy. I did this for two months, having sex with both of them, having no idea what I was going to do.

IT'S COMPLICATED - WINSTON

Sex with Winston was exciting and new, making it very different. I think he must have taken a course on how to please a woman to reach orgasm. It's funny, looking back I know I enjoyed the sex, but we weren't making love. It was mechanical on his end. I think he must have had a checklist in his head of the things he needed to do.

I remember one afternoon we were together and everything seemed to explode inside my body, maybe it was the G spot, I don't know. I remember asking him afterwards never to do that again, I didn't like it.

"How can you say you didn't like it?" he asked, flabbergasted.

"I'm not with you just to have an orgasm. I don't know what the fuck that was, but I know I didn't like it," I responded back.

"Women want their orgasms to be intense . . . to let their whole body release . . . " I took my hand and covered his mouth to stop him from talking.

"Look Winston, I don't know what your sex life was with your wife. I'm not your wife, and I didn't like it. So if you're going to be with me, be with me. I don't need a sex instructor, can we just enjoy being together?" I asked.

He shook his head and said, "I promise I won't ever do that again."

IT'S COMPLICATED - JOE

Now, with Joe . . . well, I couldn't trust Joe. I think that's why I was always so relaxed with him because there was no pressure; it just felt natural and easy. Everyone in the office knew that I was dating Winston, only a few of the girls knew about Joe. I decided I was going to have my family meet both of them and bring them into my daughters' lives. I couldn't make a decision. I was leaving it all to faith.

Joe had dinner with my mother, she loves jewelry, she was wearing an initial M diamond ring and Joe remarked on how beautiful it was. Of course my mother responded that my sister would be getting it when she dies, because her name is Marion, indicating that I wouldn't have one.

On my next date night with Joe, he surprised me with the gigantic diamond E initial ring. I looked at it and thanked him. He was excited, thinking that I was going to love it. I didn't have the heart to tell him that I hated it. I went to work the next day and showed Lorraine and Victoria.

"Oh no!" they giggled, "He wants to make you a guidette!" We were laughing so hard.

"It's horrible, I can't wear this," I told them honestly.

The next night I explained to Joe that the ring was too big and I would never wear it on my finger. Maybe as a necklace it would look good, but the truth was I wasn't ready yet to make a commitment to him. This affected him more than I realized, because a few days later we went to an Italian restaurant, Joe loved to drag out dinner. This particular night he had a few too many drinks in him. When we got home he was acting very strange, after coming out of the bathroom, I found him sitting on the bed staring at the wall.

"I'm not sleeping with you tonight, you are just using me for sex. You never tell me that you love me," he said, seriously. I began laughing nervously, knowing that I really wanted to be with him. *It is time to tell him, Ellie!* I thought.

"J-Joe, don't be silly. Y-you know that I love you. I wouldn't be here if I didn't," I told him softly. He reached out for me and we made love. Afterwards I jokingly told him that I had lied and I just wanted to get laid, we laughed together, neither of us really knowing what the real truth was. Later I put my clothes on and left to go home.

IT'S COMPLICATED - WINSTON

Winston wanted me to become his partner in everything. Our relationship was more geared around business. He wanted to buy a building in Manhattan and it was going to be a co-op business where services were shared. On my Thursdays off we would go into Manhattan and view various buildings, He wanted to make me a partner in every deal he was involved with.

Danielle often questioned me as to what I was doing.

"Does Winston know that you have no money and live in the projects?" She asked.

"I haven't told him that part yet," I joked.

We would laugh about my Winston adventures. At this time I cared about nothing. I was going wherever the wind would take me. I would come home and talk with Danielle about both of them.

When our sales agent, Bobby, was to be married, Winston and I were invited. Victoria went with Armani. The wedding was on the same day as Tom's 30th birthday party. Normally, I would not be invited to Tom's home, but Winston had been invited. Much to Jenny's dissatisfaction I happened to be Winston's date. We stopped by his house briefly to wish him a Happy Birthday.

We were all dressed for the wedding and I looked pretty damn good, even if I say so myself. Maybe it was Winston, he made me feel beautiful in anything I wore. We were all sitting in the backyard when Tom came over, and he stared at me.

"You look beautiful!" he told me. Jenny quickly glared at me. I didn't get a chance to respond before Winston said

"Thank you! Ellie dressed me." Winston had honestly thought the compliment was for him.

Jenny laughed and everyone started laughing. Tom kept staring at me and asked me if I would like to see the house. Winston popped right up.

"Of course we do," he acknowledged.

I don't think Tom was actually inviting Winston for the tour of the house. Tom was different today, he really wanted to go to the wedding, but Jenny made her plans to have his birthday party on the same day.

Prior to this home, Tom had purchased a home in Westchester. They only lived there a couple of months because Jenny had hated it there. Tom was upset, and in a conversation we had a few months earlier, he told me that he was done, he wasn't going to make himself crazy trying to please her, so they purchased this townhouse.

Tom looked different today; maybe because this was the first time I had seen him in his home environment. We eventually had to leave, Tom thanked us for coming and when he went to kiss me goodbye, he whispered in my ear.

"You look so happy," I smiled back at him, and looked over to Winston.

"I am, thanks. He may be a little out there, but he makes me feel beautiful," I said.

"That's because you are," Tom whispered. I was shocked, and maybe it was the way he looked at me when he said those words, I felt something inside that I could not explain.

We went off to the wedding and I felt like a princess. There was a popular song out called "Lady in Red" at that time. I was wearing pink that night so it wasn't the color of the dress, but the words to the song. Winston constantly played it and told me that was how he felt whenever he was with me. He told everyone how happy he was to be with me. I never had someone openly praise me like that. I liked it very much.

IT'S COMPLICATED - TOM

One afternoon, I went out to lunch with Joe at the steakhouse right up the block. I hadn't been gone longer that an hour. When I walked into the office Catherine told me that Tom was pissed off. I decided not to go in there, but he had heard my voice and came out of his office screaming at me.

"I beeped you, do you know how many times I beeped you?" He questioned.

"Why do you have a beeper if you don't call me back? I don't pay you to go to lunch with other men. Do that on your own time, not on mine," he was on a tirade.

"You didn't beep me. I would have called you and what's the big deal?" I asked, looking at his crazy eyes.

"Give me the beeper, give me that beeper?" he demanded.

I gave it to him and he placed it on the desk in front of Catherine.

"Call her number . . . you heard me . . . call her number," he ordered.

We all stood watching as Catherine called me. The beeper didn't go off. I looked at him, picked up the beeper and handed it to him.

"Keep your fucking beeper," I yelled, and walked to my desk to resume work.

I heard him in his office muttering and grumbling and shortly thereafter he left. When his car pulled away, everyone got up from their desk and came by me, they felt that Tom was jealous and they began teasing me.

"Is mommy cheating on daddy?" They would say.

We had earned these roles over the years. Tom was like the dad, who did not always come into work in a good mood, and if mommy wasn't around his mood got worse. It became a habit that when I came in, the girls would comment how daddy was in a really bad mood. I would immediately walk into his office and ask him if he had eaten (like a good mommy).

I was aware that Tom was drinking a lot trying to keep up with Jimmy and Richard and it was taking a toll on him along with all his personal problems. We had stopped our breakfast meetings together and I missed that. I think he did as well, as they seemed to relax him. When he got like this I would get him orange juice or something to eat, and we talked about anything and everything. Usually within a few minutes he would be okay. When Tom wasn't there the office had a free-for-all, everybody laughed and would joke around, but as soon as Catherine gave the word that Tom was coming, everyone would run back to their desk, pick up the phones as if they had been working hard.

Another fun, but strange day with Tom and the other agents, was during an advertising campaign. Frannie had a family photography business and we all went to the studio to have group pictures taken and individual shots for advertising. Everyone was joking, but clearly insinuating that Tom and I wanted to be with each other. They got a little out of hand, teasing him saying he was looking down my blouse. Frannie's husband carried on the joke telling Tom to look into my eyes. When Tom did look into my eyes, I felt chills going down my whole body. I didn't know what that meant, but I could not deal with another man right now, I had too much on my plate. I decided to ignore the situation. Tom had no idea what was truly going on in the office.

IT'S COMPLICATED – THE OFFICE STAFF

Catherine, the day secretary, was involved with one of the partner's friends and a friend of Tom's father. Cathy, the night secretary was sleeping with Rocco, an owner of one of the stores in the shopping center, and also a mortgage broker. Victoria was secretly seeing Armani.

Then there was Maggie who slept with anyone—Sophia finally called me to come into the office, something was really wrong. Maggie would leave looking really good, but when she returned with a signed contract, her hair was messed and her clothes were all out place.

The following Sunday I followed her, she went into the Staten Island Hotel, where she met a client. I saw her go in, and then about an hour later she came out. I saw for myself what she was up to. I waited in the office until she returned. I called her in and explained that what she was doing was not the way to sell real estate. I warned her that Tom would not like to think he was running a house of prostitution. Later that week, I learned that Cathy had sex on the conference room table with the mortgage broker. My God!

Every time we had a meeting after that I could not erase the memory. Victoria would come in with Lysol to clean the table and say "You never know" and we all started laughing. Tom had no idea what we were laughing about. I did my campaign with all the agents to get their names out there, hoping that someone would call in and list their houses. I spotlighted one agent a month. When it came time for Frannie the woman whose family owned the photography studio, Frannie immediately had a call come in regarding her profile.

She picked up the phone.

"You disgusting pig!" we heard.

When she came out of the office she was furious.

"He said I looked like I would give a good blow job!" she was horrified.

All day Frannie would look in the mirror at her mouth. We couldn't believe it when she asked every man who walked in if she looked like the type of person who gives a good blowjob. Tom was shocked at first when she asked him. We were very surprised when he got on the bandwagon and started slinging the jokes. He liked her and could joke around with her the most. It lightened things up.

There are so many stories like Frannie's. Lorraine took care of all the Chinese clients. If they were Chinese or couldn't speak English, give them to Lorraine that was the joke in the office.

Victoria was in a world of her own, she worked hard and only wanted the big deals, and she got them through blood, sweat and tears. I remember only a year before how excited she became getting an apartment rental. She liked the commercial side of real estate, and not the residential. She didn't like having to listen to the whims of the wives not knowing what they wanted. She liked getting the listings and having other agents sell them. By this time the office was full of agents.

Bobby and George came in during the evenings. Those nights were the funniest. George reminded me of Bruce Willis in the show

Moonlighting. It was a television series at the time. We had a good time with this and every time George and I would go on a listing, people commented on the resemblance, George would interrupt them and jokingly call me Sybil and introduce himself as Bruce.

With this group you could not have a serious meeting. I introduced role playing exercises and in one meeting it got totally out of control. I set up scenarios about homeowners and they would have to improvise on what they would do in each situation. It should have been training exercises, but instead we were like children around the table playing a game.

The first scenario:
You get a call from the wife to come list the house, when the husband opens the door, he in his pajamas. What do you say?
That question was given to George. He replied, *"Nice Pajamas"* and stuck out his hand like comedians do after telling a joke that starts the night.
The next scenario went to Bobby.
You're going to list a house and you just found out his wife has passed away. How do you handle this listing?
Bobby started*: "Sir I am really sorry for your loss and I know this must be a hard time for you* . . . as he was trying to speak Victoria was in the background making sounds like a dead wife haunting the house.
The entire meeting went that way and the next day we were all talking about the fun we had. Tom commented that he would have liked to have been there. I think he struggled with being the owner, and really did know his place. He wasn't like Richard and Jimmy. He truly wanted to be with us, but being the boss there was a line he couldn't cross.

IT'S COMPLICATED – JOE

Now, back to my saga with Joe.
Winston kept pushing me to go to St. John's with him. I explained that it wouldn't be right, given that I was still seeing Joe.

"What if Joe didn't know that you were going with me? What if you were going on vacation with Victoria?" He suggested. He offered to pay for Victoria to go on vacation with us. I think he thought that if I went to St. John's with him, I would fall madly in love and forget Joe.

My family was no help. I took Joe to my niece's communion party and my father called him Winston.

"No, that's the other guy," Joe responded.

When I took Winston to a concert, my mother's friend commented as we were leaving that it was nice meeting you Frank. Winston looked at me.

"I know that there is a Joe, but is there also a Frank?" he asked, seriously.

"There is no Frank!" I quickly told him.

My mother, Marie, and I burst up laughing, and my father's advice was to marry Winston and fool around with Joe. My mother didn't like Winston because he wore brown shoes. The girls in the office said if you choose Joe you'll be working for the rest of your life.

My Joy loved Winston, or I should say she liked what Winston could buy her, and Dawn hated him. She just didn't like him. Now Joe on the other hand she loved, she would call him "MY JOE".

Joe loved both of them, but Dawn found her love in Joe, probably because he was so childish himself. Dawn was graduating from kindergarten, and Joe would talk about this store in his neighborhood in Brooklyn that sold beautiful dresses. He offered to buy Dawn her graduation dress. Most kindergarten graduation dresses are usually plain cotton dresses, well Dawn was his guidette, and they were two peas in a pod. She came home with this off the shoulder, lace ruffled dress, with matching shoes. I think he even bought her a tiara. That day I looked at the two of them, and I knew he was the one!

IT'S COMPLICATED – WINSTON'S ISLAND

I already had my vacation planned with Winston. After I told him about my feelings for Joe, he insisted that we still go on the vacation.

"Please Ellie, come with me and when you get back if you choose to be with Joe, I will understand. I really want you to see the island," he insisted.

I lied to Joe and when he offered to watch my dog, I felt like shit. I don't know why I lied, and Joe knew I had planned on making my decision after July. But he kept pushing me, and the more he pushed that only kept Winston in my life. He wasn't listening to me. I knew I was going to hurt somebody and for the first time it wasn't going to be me.

St. John's here we come! Winston rented a beautiful, two-bedroom house on the mountainside; it had a deck with the most amazing view. This was truly a beautiful island. Winston knew everyone. He knew the woman who owned over 50% of the island, so we weren't tourists. We went to every secluded beach on the island with her permission. It could have been beautiful, but poor Victoria (who had come with us) found nobody around, every beach was secluded it was just the three of us.

The first day we went shopping, which meant taking a boat to the main island and bringing our groceries back on a boat. It was an adventure. Then when Winston rented a stick shift Jeep, every day when we would leave to go somewhere, we were attacked by wild dogs driving down the mountain.

Victoria and Winston liked to drink and made me the designated driver, which would not have been bad if I knew how to drive a stick shift. One afternoon, after the beach and lunch, we stopped to smoke a joint. The problem was, not only could I not drive a stick shift, but now I was stoned. Winston and Victoria were totally wasted. Driving around tight mountain curves was scary, because these roads had no guardrails. Suddenly the car slipped a gear and we were going down the road in reverse.

It was like a scene from a movie, but this was real. Victoria was in the back seat screaming, "Oh my God. Oh my God!" The two back wheels of the jeep were an inch off solid ground, we found ourselves hanging off the cliff. We probably would have died if I hadn't smoked that joint, instantly I saw the funny side and started laughing.

"No problem folks, I can do this!" I told them. Winston and Victoria were yelling and screaming for me not to move. Without even thinking I shifted gears and the Jeep moved forward. I did it! I don't know how, but we were still there. Everyone sobered up real quick after that.

On the third day of the vacation we went to our second secluded beach. On the previous day we had to deal with a donkey on the beach. Winston and I were in the water and heard Victoria screaming at the top of her voice.

"That's it! I've had enough. I can't take this any longer."

We quickly looked down at the shore and a wild boar was actually chasing Victoria. She was waving her hands above her head running into the water and screaming

"Help! Help me. This is fucking ridiculous. I want to go to a beach where there are people, not donkeys and pigs," she was ranting. "This may be romantic for you, but I would like to get laid. Take me to a beach where there are people p-please?" She was at her wits end.

Winston and I couldn't stop laughing, even today I can see Victoria running away from the pig and I still laugh out loud.

The next day Winston packed a picnic basket and we finally went to a beach with people. When we decided to eat lunch Winston pointed to an alcove over to the right.

"Look at that beautiful secluded section, would you like to eat there?" he suggested.

"Winston let's just eat here," I said, impatiently.

He insisted on how beautiful the spot was and then I lost it.

"We have had seclusion for the last three days. I am fine here. I just want to eat!" I screamed.

He ignored me and slowly bent down to give Victoria our sandwiches.

"Fine! I'll go by myself," he said, skipping away with his basket.

I looked at Victoria. She was holding in her laughter.

"He's not for me, look at him," I said pointing at him.

With that we went into hysterics looking at this man skipping away with his little basket.

Victoria finally met someone, and the next few days Winston and I were on our own. He took me to his property and to his neighbor's house near the property—the home was gorgeous. I had never seen a home like this. Marble was everywhere, and there were no doors at the back of the house due to the fact that it was built on a mountain.

When we went out on the balcony, Winston was pointing to his property asking me what design I would like.

"I don't know, but what I do know . . . I would like some doors."

"It is very safe without doors," he explained.

"What about the bugs, boars, donkeys, and stray dogs? Sorry, I want a home with doors. They can be glass doors, I don't care but I need doors," I told him, and for a few minutes this was truly a fantasy.

Who was I kidding? I wasn't going to move my daughters to this island. I wasn't moving away from everyone, a vacation home maybe. Winston was a dreamer, and he saw the two us living in his home, on this island, madly in love until the day we died. The problem was I liked him, but I was not in love with him. The rest of the vacation was beautiful and I enjoyed every moment.

But, when it was time to leave, we were running late. Catching the plane home was a fiasco. The airline held the plane for us, but we were faced with irate passengers. Victoria and I were laughing and acting ridiculous, being totally irresponsible. One passenger came up from behind and grabbed Victoria by the shirt.

"If the two of you don't stop, I think I may kill the both of you," he hissed.

We smiled quietly to each other and took our seats. The plane took off and I began to doze off, Winston thought I was sleeping and he began talking to Victoria.

"I know she is going back to Joe," he said.

"I really don't know what Ellie will do," she told him, but Victoria knew.

MY FINAL DANCE WITH JOE

The next day I visited Joe to pick up my dog, we talked about the vacation, but of course I left out the Winston part. Afterward I went to work for the day and everything was fine. When I got home Joe called and started screaming at me.

"Ellie, I just got a phone call from a person who said that you went on vacation with Winston. Were you?" he asked.

"Yes, I'm not going lie. I asked you to give me until the month of July, but you wouldn't stop, you kept pushing me, so I did what I had to do. Sorry Joe," I said, hanging up the phone.

I immediately called Victoria and was shocked by her response.

"What are you still doing in the house?" She screamed, "get the fuck out of there, he's going to come to your house and he may kill you. He just found out that you went on vacation with another man, get the fuck out of there," Victoria warned me.

"Stop it," I said, "Joe's not going to do anything to me. He is at work."

"I know what I'm talking about, call his office. I guarantee you he's not there. He's on his way to your house," Victoria insisted.

I hung up the phone and called Joe's office, it went right to the answering machine, I remember thinking. *Oh shit, Victoria was right!* I called my mother to see if my brother Mikie was home, I wanted him to come over. She put him on the phone.

"Are you serious?" Mikie asked.

"Yes, he could kill me," I explained.

"Get out of the house, I'll be right there," Mikie told me.

I immediately tried to get out of the house, but in my panic I couldn't find my keys. Frantically searching, I finally found them and headed for my car and got in and started the car. To my surprise Joe's car was suddenly blocking the driver's side of my car. I couldn't get away and I began yelling.

"Go away, just go away!"

It was the first time in my life I was truly scared of a man. Then my brother Mikie pulled up behind me and got out of his car.

"Calm down. Everyone calm down," he said to us.

People everywhere were watching the commotion. I could hear Joe and my brother arguing. I looked over to my right and there was Danielle standing behind the tree. She popped her head out and mouthed their names pointing to Joe and my brother. She thought Mikie was Winston. I shook my head laughing, no. She ran her hand across her forehead indicating "Phew".

Once I saw Danielle I laughed, and knowing that my brother was there, I wasn't afraid anymore. I vividly remember Joe's face at the window yelling at me. I kept squinting my eyes and turned my head away every time. For the first time in my life I did deserve to get yelled at. I had been bad and it was wrong. Mikie calmed things down and finally got Joe to leave quietly.

That day changed everything. It bothered me a lot the way Joe had acted. Unfortunately, the next time I saw him he was drunk, mean drunk! After Mark this was something I could not handle. Maybe this was the real Joe? We argued the whole night and I finally said what I needed to.

"How does it feel to be lied to, cheated on, and embarrassed? You got engaged, and you left me alone for my 30th birthday, without even calling. Was I just supposed to forget everything, because you suddenly decide that you want me?" I screamed at him.

It felt good to get all this hurt off my chest, he didn't say a word and I continued.

"After years of this bullshit, I'm sorry Joe, all we do is hurt each other and I have never done anything like this is my life to anyone. You bring out the worst in me and I don't like it."

"Can you forgive me?" he asked.

"No," I replied, adamantly.

"Even Jesus Christ forgave," he whimpered, thinking that comment would get me to come around.

"Joe, let's just say that Jesus Christ is nicer than me, okay? I know I can't forgive you, but I also think that I'll never forget you either. Bye Joe!" I said, and walked out the door. I got into my car crying. I don't know why, but I drove to Winston's house. He was so surprised to see me, I was a wreck and I told him everything that happened between Joe and myself. Then he looked at me.

"I thought I was never going to see you again," he admitted.

We talked for a while about a lot of things.

"I'm glad you finally opened your eyes, Joe has hurt you too many times." Winston then went on to tell me how crazy in love he was with me.

"I know you don't feel it right now, but we can have a normal relationship, be more involved in each other's lives, go out with friends and be a couple. I promise I will make you happy," he declared.

"A year from now everything will be different, you'll see," Winston said. I just nodded my head despondently.

I left his house that night knowing everything he said was probably right for me. Joe was out of my life. The worse part was when I had to tell Dawn that Joe was not going to be part of our lives.

She cried when I told her and ran in her room. She took out her graduation dress and cried into the fabric, "My Joe, My Joe!"

I sat there crying with her, hoping that I had made the right decision.

CHAPTER ELEVEN

INTRIGUE

Now that Joe was out of my life, I needed to finalize my marriage with Mark. I called him to discuss a divorce, it just so happened that on our tenth anniversary we went to the attorney and signed the papers. I took out the Cobra policy so I would have my own medical insurance. We used my friend, who is an attorney. I didn't want to fight any longer. I gave Mark his pension, and the only thing we argued about was his life insurance. I wanted my daughters to be the beneficiaries, not his father.

The attorney persuaded him to agree, which Mark did. In fact he could not believe how cordial our divorce was when Mark told him he was taking me out to dinner. The attorney thought we were a great couple. Mark made reservations at an expensive restaurant, and to my surprise when we arrived at the table there were a dozen roses. Then he had the accordion player come to the table.

The way we were. He started playing.

"You have to be kidding me?" I was astounded.

"I just want you to remember what you're going to be missing," he said, seriously. He actually believed that I was going to miss this?

"If you would have done this when we were married, maybe we wouldn't be sitting here tonight, asshole," I responded, nicely.

He just shook his head in a typical Mark fashion. We had a lovely dinner and then he drove back to the attorney's office to pick up my car. We sat in the car for a while listening to some songs on the radio and reminiscing over the past, mostly the good times, then we hugged and I left. It was over!

I remember driving home and was surprised that I didn't cry. I always cried. I was relieved, no more looking back only forward.

That evening I wrote this poem:

The Wind

> I look at all the clouds in the sky
> Sometimes drifting and living alone
> Depressed and full of sorrow
> Waiting for the dark sky to appear
> So I can release my tears
> Then the sky turns blue and the clouds surround me
> The sun appears smiling and shining
> A new day and I am proud
> I am soft loving and gay
> I am wisped across the sky with a smile all the way
> Soon the wind will come and I will change again
> I'll see the dark skies I'll see the blue skies
> I'll see many seasons and magnificent views
> But I'll never forget that it is the wind
> That always pulls me through.

My life with Winston wasn't so wonderful, because he was so insecure. His wife had cheated on him and now he was not only supporting his wife and two children, but also her boyfriend. Winston was a man I couldn't respect, because he let his wife walk all over him. Before his wife left his home, he was living in the house with her boyfriend. I could never understand why a man would put himself through something like that.

He didn't care about his appearance but I did. He had the money and there was no reason for him to walk around dressed that way. He was a successful businessman and should look like one. One day we went to Barney's in New York, we purchased one black, blue, and brown suit as well as numerous shirts, ties, and shoes to match. *Pretty Woman* in reverse, but he was paying for the clothes.

Work was still moving forward. Many new and exciting things were happening now that we were selling homes in Florida. Brian brought a builder from Florida, and we ran seminars in Staten Island for the new sales team that came up from Florida.

Again new faces and new beginnings, but now everything changed. I wasn't treated as a secretary and office manager given that I was seeing Winston. I was more involved with everything as if I was a partner. During this time Tom and I became close again, all the years he was my only constant, but during the times we drifted away from each other, we always returned.

Tom's office had a window that faced my desk. So through the years, sometimes I would just stand and look at his desk to see if he was there. He would do the same. Sometimes we would catch each other doing this. Always we came up with an excuse so as not to be embarrassed. He was my security. Tom saw the change in me and I think he liked it, but he was changing also. He was different, he stared at me a lot more now and we had more personal conversations, which we hadn't had in the past.

I remember one night I slept at Winston's house, the office had a scheduled meeting with the sales team from Florida, I had brought a change of clothes. I woke up late with no time to dress for the office. I had Winston drive me to work. I rushed in the office and every one was there. Tom came out.

"We are waiting for you, Ellie," he smiled. I pointed my finger towards the bathroom.

"I'm going to change. I'll be right there," I said looking guilty.

I went to get my skirt and it was missing, either I had left it in the car or in Winston's house. I crept out of the bathroom and asked Cathy to get Tom. I stuck my head out and told him I had lost my skirt. I was going to run up to the boutique in the shopping center and buy an outfit and could he stall the meeting? I bought and put on the outfit, I wasn't even gone fifteen minutes. As soon as I walked into the meeting Tom just shook his head and started smiling. The meeting went well. The old Tom probably would have yelled at me, but not this Tom. He was amused by my antics.

After the meeting all the agents left and Tom looked at me grinning.

"You're amazing, not only do you shop for an outfit in five minutes, but you even accessorize the outfit. You look beautiful and I really like your choice," he said and walked out.

We were planning on having a seminar. I wrote the speeches for everyone, went to the reception room to lay out the floor plan, did all the advertising and sat in on the strategy meetings. I loved my job, and it was so diversified. I never did the same thing two days in a row. I followed up on the pending deals and was always there to assist the agents, but give me a new project and I would give 150%.

During the writing of all the speeches, Tom approached me.

"Why aren't you writing one for yourself?" he asked.

"Not me, Tom, I like being in background. I don't want to disappoint you, let me do what I am good at, okay?" I asked.

He smiled and understood me completely.

Winston came to the seminar looking rather handsome in his suit. I will say that the seminar was most successful. At the end of the evening, Tom read his speech exactly as I had written it with one exception, he publicly acknowledged me.

"I would like everyone to turn around and thank Ellie, for all her hard work and for making tonight a success. It's not just what she did here tonight, but what she does every day."

Everyone in the room instantly applauded. Tom wanted me to come to the stage, but I shook my head, no. I realized that I was in love with him. No one in my life had ever appreciated the things I did. He not only appreciated me, but he publicly announced it. I was changing, different feelings were coming out and I didn't know what to do with them.

The Florida sales agents were crazy. Every time they came in, it was a party and everyone got drunk. They would go to Manhattan and do all sorts of crazy things. Winston would go with them, he would invite me, but it wasn't for me. I encouraged him to go with the guys, as I felt he needed to do that.

WINSTON'S INSECURITIES

Armani, Victoria, Winston and I went out one night to a club in Manhattan. Victoria and I love to dance, and we were a little crazy. We would get on the dance floor and just forget that people were watching us. In our minds, why would anyone watch us? We didn't think we were great dancers. As we walked off the dance floor we could see that Winston looked angry.

"What bug is up his ass?" Victoria asked me.

"I have no idea."

As I approached the table Winston stood up and announced,

"Ellie, we are leaving. Did you have fun performing for everyone? Did you know that everyone was staring? I see you enjoy performing sexual dances for strangers." he bellowed.

As soon he said sexual dances, Victoria and I burst out laughing. I laughed right in his face and let him have it.

"How dare you . . . you little, pathetic, insecure man. The way I danced just now is the same way I danced with you four months ago. Remember your fucking song?" I was pissed. "The Lady in Red!" I yelled. "How honored you were to be with me back then, the only difference now is that you think you own me, and I should act the way you want me to."

"Keep your voice down," Winston motioned, he was turning red and so he should. I continued.

"Do you want a little wimp who sits by your side and watches people dance? Well, sorry that will never be me. I love, love, to dance. Not you, not anybody, will take that away from me. What you could have said was that you love watching me dance, or that you are thrilled other men are looking at me." Victoria tried to gently quiet me, but I was all riled up. "Or you could have said how great it is to be going home with me," I screamed in his face in front of everyone. "You didn't say any of that Winston . . . and now, you are going home alone." I grabbed Victoria and we left, as we were walking down the street when Victoria reminded me of another time in my past.

"Remember the night someone called you a wimp when you danced? Boy, girl you have come along way," she said. "Did he say that we were performing sexual dances for strangers, did you see a pole?" she asked, and we laughed.

"Were we dancing on poles? We were fucking dancing! Was I grinding you, was I thrusting you? What the fuck did we do?" Victoria was more upset then me. She was pushing her pelvis in and out, mocking a dance move.

"Did I do this?" she asked. All I could do was laugh, Winston was a fool and this was so ridiculous. I never saw Victoria so angry and insulted. I don't remember how we got home that night, but I do remember Victoria asking if I wanted to go back to the club.

"Ellie, we could go back and dance another set. Apparently we could get very lucky in there, with all those men lusting after us," she said, opening her mouth and sticking out her tongue, imitating a dog in heat. Thank God for Victoria, she took a ridiculous evening and made it so much fun. We didn't go back into the club and I didn't speak with Winston for a few days, I could see that Winston was changing.

He owned a beautiful home with a gorgeous kitchen. I would have loved living in that home, but there was one problem. Winston couldn't stop pushing me to be with him. I had a full time job and two daughters to raise. I didn't want him in my life every night, I wanted time to be with my children alone, but he never listened and always showed up with dinner, telling me he didn't want me to have to cook, he just never listened. I loved to cook for my kids!

It had been nine months, and I had to go back into the hospital and get off my Dancorine. What a crazy nine months, I realized I did all these things on this medication. I acted like a man. In those nine months I did whatever I wanted to do, just like a man.

Winston offered his home for me to recuperate after my surgery. When I got home there were flowers waiting for me. Winston knew I loved flowers, and he would buy me books on exotic flowers suggesting that we could plant them on St. John's Island. Well, these weren't flowers I liked, they looked more like a funeral arrangement. It was funny, when Danielle brought my girls to see me at his house the first thing I asked her was to check out my flowers. I remember she came into the kitchen and wanted to know who had died.

"Do you see what I am talking about? He's not normal," I said, shaking my head.

"He tries too hard the poor guy," Danielle felt sorry for him.

"You are exactly right."

That day the girls were in his house, Danielle had also brought her daughter, Casey, there was a bunch of girls all running around. The home was large and their voices echoed, but when I saw Winston's reaction to them, I knew right there and then he was not the one for me. He seemed annoyed with the girls playing and kept saying to me that I needed my rest. It was rattling him. Basically, he was chasing my children out of his house. This was another argument we would have.

I left his home the next day and said I would be fine on my own. When I went back to work I saw everyone talking, something just didn't seem right. Nine months earlier we opened a second office and Teresa was the manager. For the past few weeks Tom was talking about changing to a franchised real estate company, which was a new concept, more like sharing office services and agents being responsible for splitting the costs.

I didn't understand the concept and he didn't talk enough about it for me to understand. Teresa was in Tom's office, which was surprising to me. When she left she had a strange look on her face. Tom left right after her and I asked Cathy what was going on. She suggested that I speak with Teresa. I went to her office and I guess she thought I knew, (which I didn't) apparently I was being fired and Teresa was the new office manager for the new franchise that they were buying into.

While I was sitting in Teresa's office, apparently she called Tom because I was so upset. Tom walked into the room and looked at me,

"I didn't want you to find out this way. I wanted to tell you myself." I went crazy and I was hysterical.

"How could you do this to me?" I kept repeating it. He calmed me down and explained that it was not his idea. He was against it, but they wouldn't listen to him. Richard and Jimmy wanted me out. Tom for some reason thought I was going to leave because of my relationship with Winston.

"What does Winston have to do with this?" I asked.

"Winston is always bragging about the various business ventures you will be undertaking."

"Winston lives in a dream world," I responded, "I had no intention of leaving, I built this company with you, how could you do this to me?"

Tom said a lot, I really don't remember everything, but he set up a meeting immediately at a restaurant with Jimmy and me. In all the years Jimmy had never seen me buckle under the pressure with anything. Today was different, and I was a mess. I was crying and fighting for my job.

"It wasn't me," Jimmy said, "Richard wants you out. Tom had nothing to do with this, and he fought for you. But, Richard has it out for you and I don't know why?"

"I don't know why either," I cried.

"I have nothing against you, our company is a success. Looking at where we are today, you are a main contributor in that. We could hire you back right now, you have mine and Tom's vote, but I would like a unanimous agreement with all three of us."

"How do we do that?" I asked.

"I would like you to confront Richard on why he wants you terminated." Jimmy said. Then the three of us had a strategy meeting.

"I wouldn't meet today you are too emotional," Jimmy said. "We will set the meeting for Wednesday morning, give yourself time to prepare. Richard will not know that we have met today, and we won't tell him that you'll be coming."

I calmed down and Tom drove me to the office. I picked up some files for my presentation. I went to Winston's house that evening. I wanted to work on my presentation, but he was bothering me. I knew Winston would have been very happy if I lost my job. That would open the door for him to go into business with me.

As I was sitting there I suddenly remembered that only a couple of weeks before going out to dinner in New Jersey, Winston was showing me a development that his architect had built. It was in New Jersey right on the water. The units were priced over one million dollars each. We got out of the car to walk around. Then we heard someone calling and it was the architect who lived in one of the units. They invited us into their unit, and it was a beautiful three story with a private elevator. I really enjoyed his wife, they asked us to stay and have dinner with them. I went into the kitchen with the wife and we heated all kinds of leftovers, everyone got drunk and we had a great time.

The next day, Winston called me and asked me if I liked the condo and of course I said that I did. Then in the next breath he told me he was buying one for me.

"The Walden's loved you and they want you to work with them. If you had a place in New Jersey you could work there," he said. "I have known the Walden's for over five years and had never been invited out socially with them, now they want us to go sailing with them this weekend." I was surprised.

"Slow down, Winston, they were nice people. Firstly you are not buying me a condo, and secondly I am not working for the Walden's. I have a job which I love and I'm not moving my children to New Jersey. If you want to go sailing with them, I don't have a problem with that," I told him straight and we never discussed it again. But, I couldn't help but wonder if Tom knew about this.

The next day I was driving to meet Tom before the presentation. I had a moment to think about everything and why I was so upset. It wasn't so much the job, in the past few years I had been offered numerous positions, even Mr. Wallace from Manhattan offered me a job. It was Tom, not seeing him on a daily basis hurt. I didn't cry for losing my job, I cried because I was going to lose Tom. I needed him, and he had been my strength over the years. He had made me this independent, free, and confident woman.

I thought back to the first time we met and how shy I was. How he had brought out a different side of me just by believing in me. No one had ever believed in me. Oh my God. I had fallen in love with him, and maybe I shouldn't fight to get my job back. Maybe some one is trying to tell me something, I should just tell Tom to leave it the way it is. Let Teresa take the job. When I pulled up to the office, Tom came walking out and he looked at me, the moment I saw his smile, I knew I wasn't strong enough to leave him. We drove to the meeting and walked in together. Richard was surprised to see me, and Jimmy acted like he had no idea why I was there.

Tom started the meeting by saying that he had discussed the situation with me and he wanted to address their decision to terminate my employment. He would like to have me state my case, and after they heard what I had to say, only then should they make the decision as to who was the right person to be the manager of the franchise. I sat down at the conference table right across from Jimmy and Richard. Tom sat beside me. I started the meeting saying that I had four questions to ask.

1) Was I being terminated for not doing my job?
2) Do any of them know what my job is?
3) Can any of them tell me my job description?
4) What duties have I performed for this company in the last three years?

No one could answer.

"So I am being fired from a job that no one knows what the job is. That's why I am here today? You opened another office less than a year ago, and the person you are replacing me with is Teresa, the other office manager. She started at her office with all of my agents whom I trained. She has not hired one new agent. That office is not making money. My office carries her office. No one gave me a job description, Tom promoted me to office manager and I made up the job as I went along."

My throat was dry, so I took a sip of water before I continued.

"Let me ask you, what two things do you need in real estate? Agents and advertising, right? I recruited every agent and I trained every agent. All advertising and budgeting goes through me. Every deal that is made in both offices is followed up by me!"

Richard started to squirm in his chair. I looked over at Tom and only saw admiration in his eyes. I continued.

"Once my agents bring in a signed contract I take over every deal until closing—the banks, attorneys, buyers and sellers. We have a 95 % closing rate in this office. No real estate office has that. I was the one to implement weekly office meetings, incentives and training programs. I did them to run this business successfully. Other real estate offices have three different divisions doing what I do."

I paused and looked at each of them slowly. I was about to close.

"I think we know that it is not my job performance that is the problem. I think the problem is personal," I said looking right at Richard. "Is that right Richard?" I asked.

Richard just put his head down and he didn't say a word.

"Tom and Jimmy, could you please leave the room because I need to speak with Richard alone?" I asked.

Tom and Jimmy jumped right up and left the room. Now it was just Richard and me. He was the biggest liar in the world.

"No, Ellie. No, it's not personal. It's all the stuff I've been hearing about you and Winston. You are never in the office, and you . . ." I stopped him.

"It's personal because of Joe, right?" I asked, and I got no answer so I continued.

"My personal relationships have nothing to do with my job performance. If your friend is hurt, that is not my problem."

I knew how revengeful and spiteful Joe could be, but let's face it he made his bed last year when he got engaged to Stella. I thought I could get past it, but I couldn't. Yes, I have someone in my life, but I should not lose my job for that. Richard apologized and he offered to bury the hatchet. I agreed and I kept my job.

Driving back to the office with Tom was great, and he was like a little kid repeating the events of the meeting. He recalled the best moment was when I said it was personal, and went on to ask them to leave the room because I needed to speak with Richard alone! It was great when he went on to tell me that Jimmy had the greatest respect for me and he had no idea all the things I did with my job. Tom gave me a week off, saying I deserved it after what they had put me through.

I had a week off and I was going to help Danielle remodel her apartment. I could wall paper, paint and apply stick-on tiles. I like doing physical things it clears my head. I hadn't had a week off since July. I had a few days off with my surgery, but I wanted time to be with my kids and my friends. Winston called me constantly, and he was disappointed that I didn't leave my job. It really bothered him that I was home and not making any time for him. I explained what I was doing numerous times, but he didn't listen as always. Instead he would show up every night at dinnertime. Using the excuse that he wanted to help out.

One night, wallpapering Danielle's kitchen, I was standing on the washing machine and the doorbell rang, it was Winston. I was standing there with a razorblade in my hand and he started telling me that he had bought dinner for us, apparently he had called and I wasn't home. He figured that I would be at Danielle's house.

I lost it right at that moment.

"No Winston. You knew I was here because I told you what I was doing. I told you not to come over that I would be busy, but you never listen to me," I exploded.

"I just thought I could help you," he stammered.

"I know how to put up wallpaper!"

"I wanted to help you," he repeated.

"I enjoy doing this and I don't need your help. I told you that three times today, now leave. I am really angry and I don't want to talk or see you right now, so please leave," I ordered.

He took the Chinese food he had bought, waved goodbye to Danielle and the girls, and left. When the door closed Danielle burst out laughing,

"I thought you were going to slit his throat, every time you said something to him, your hands were flailing and I just kept seeing that razorblade in your hand."

"I don't want to be mean, but the man does not listen. He keeps trying to tell me what is good for me. In that man's eyes, the only thing that is good for me is him."

I didn't realize it then, but the medicine, Danocrine, was leaving my system. My female hormones were returning, and they didn't like Winston.

One evening we attended a charity event. Victoria was modeling that evening. Winston looked very handsome. We got there early and went to the bar, Victoria's date, Charles, was there. Victoria had known Charles for years and he loved her for all that time, but he wasn't what Victoria wanted. We were around many successful men and it wasn't the money. They were interesting, smart, and exciting. Charles was just a nice guy with no real ambition.

I liked Charles a lot and when we got to the bar, I saw that he was wearing a suit that was too big for him, the sleeves hung down about one inch over his hands, and the pants were over an inch too long. Today, I would do nothing, but back then men dressed meticulously, or at least the group of men we were sitting with. I asked him if Victoria had seen him, but she had told him to meet her here. I knew if Victoria saw him dressed that way she would have been embarrassed. I asked the bartender if she had a needle and thread, no luck. Then I asked her if she had a stapler and a black magic marker. She gave them to me and I altered Charles' suit right there in the bar. It came out pretty good. He looked nice.

We got there early and went to our table. Tom and Jenny, L.P. and Laura, Jimmy and Lacy, Maxine and Bill, Winston and I and of course Charles. Victoria joined us later. This was the first time I had ever sat with any of them. I was usually put at another table, but because I was with Winston, I now belonged at this table.

I had no one to talk to except Winston and Charles. I didn't like the other girls. It was a nice evening, but I found myself looking at Tom much of the evening. I caught him doing the same, and something had changed after that meeting with Richard and Jimmy. The fashion show started and Victoria finally came out modeling lingerie, it was hysterical. She looked beautiful and I saw the way Charles looked at her, and it broke my heart.

You could see how much he loved her, and I knew Victoria did not feel the same way. The evening was better once Victoria joined us at the table. Then Winston had to ruin it again, they were modeling mink coats and he insisted that he was going to buy me one. I told him that I didn't like them, I was short and they were big and bulky. The girls across the table had overheard our conversation, they remarked on how stupid I was. Here was a man offering to buy me a mink coat and I was refusing it. They had decided that there was definitely something wrong with me.

"I don't like them, I'm little and they are bulky," I responded back. Just as I finished saying that the next coat being modeled to come out was a white ermine coat, which I had never seen before. It was sleek with short hair.

"Look at that one," Winston said. "It's not bulky." Just as he said that, the auctioneer announced that it was going for $50,000. I looked over at Winston.

"$50,000!" I mouthed.

"I don't care, you would look beautiful in it," he said.

Well, you should have seen the faces of the women at the other side of the table. Victoria burst out laughing, I looked at Tom and he looked disappointed and upset. Then I looked at Winston.

"You are not buying that coat. If you do, I will not wear it." He began to protest but I stopped him. I leaned over and spoke right in his ear.

"No! You want to buy something then go buy something for yourself. You are not buying me anything," I said, rather loudly.

Everyone at the table heard it and there was silence for few moments. I saw Tom put his hand over his mouth laughing. Then Jimmy bent over to Tom.

"I guess she told him," he said.

"That's our Ellie, she tells you like it is," Tom replied.

Then I saw Winston look towards Victoria. She smirked back.

"You have to stop pushing, you are pushing her away," she said. Victoria liked Winston and wanted me to stay with him. He made our lives interesting to say the least.

We went home that night and Winston was still upset about the coat. I knew it wasn't the coat as much as he wanted me to need him financially, and I wouldn't allow it. When we got to my apartment he started the argument.

"I know the reason why you wouldn't let me buy you the coat. It is because you don't love me anymore," he said, "I saw it tonight, you were staring at him and you are attracted to him, I think that you are going to leave me."

I couldn't believe my ears. He had seen me looking at Tom. Oh God, I was so embarrassed, what could I say to him. I was caught, he was right, there was something and maybe it was always there. I have always cared about Tom. My mind was racing.

Did Tom see it as well? I wondered if Jenny saw it, did everyone at the table see it? I thought.

I was ready to confess and then I heard.

"I saw the way you were with Charles," Winston accused.

"Charles? Are you crazy?"

"He's so handsome and you were throwing yourself all over him."

I started laughing, the relief, he didn't see anything, and nobody else did either. Now Ellie was back, I wasn't in the wrong.

"You fucking insecure idiot," I screamed at him, "that is Victoria's boyfriend who loves her with all his heart. Do you think that I would fall for a guy just because he was good looking?" I shook my head, "Did you see what I did tonight? I tried to make him look better for Victoria. I didn't want her to be embarrassed, I wanted her to feel proud when she sat down at that table with him." I stopped and thought why was I explaining all this to an idiot?

"Winston, I can't do this any longer. You are too insecure, your wife did a job on you and you are suffocating me. I think that you are a great guy, but you're too needy for me. I have a lot going on in my life and I'm being pulled in so many directions. You don't work with me, you work against me. You never listen to me and you definitely never hear me. I love my job and I love my children, and neither one is going to be leaving my life."

"Ellie, please?" he mumbled.

"The only one who is leaving is you. Now please go."

He tried to talk more, but I was so angry.

"I have a really mean and violent side to me Winston, and if you don't go now, you are going to see it. So please get the fuck out, now!" I screamed.

Lisa was also home that night and she heard our fight.

"Mom, there goes another one," she said.

CHAPTER TWELVE

❦

DREAM LAND

Winston had been out of my life for a month, it was a Sunday night, and Victoria called me in the middle of night, she and Armani were at the hospital. Apparently, it was the result of a racial attack by a group of morons. They were attacking Armani and she stepped in to defend him. I went right to the hospital, Victoria had bruises on her and Armani was beat up pretty bad. I wanted to be there for her, but then Winston walked in unexpectedly. It soon became apparent that he had come to see me. I didn't want to see him I was trying to get away from him. I saw Julio, Mark's old friend from high school.

We hadn't talked for years. He was once married to my best friend which is a very long story, well he cheated on her and left her when she was pregnant with her second child. To me he was the lowest form of human slime that was put on this earth, but it was still better than talking to Winston. Julio just happened to be the EMT driver who had responded to the call. Winston just stood there, eavesdropping on our conversation. Julio saw that I wanted to get away from him and he walked right up to Winston.

"I don't think Ellie wants you here, either go over to your friend, or please leave the hospital," he told him. Winston was not a confrontational man. He walked away and stayed with Armani. Victoria was released a little later and I took her home.

THE CHICAGO CONVENTION

That Monday I went into work. Tom, Jimmy and Richard had gone to a seminar in Chicago for the seminar. They had only been at the convention one hour when Tom called me.

"Ellie, you have to come to Chicago, we need you here. None of us know what to do, please book your flight and I'll see you tomorrow," he told me sounding panicked. "You can take the whole next week off, just be here by tomorrow," he hung up.

Now I was in a frenzy, I had to get a flight reservation, a hotel room, and of course a baby sitter. I was able to get my brother, he drove me to airport that evening, but when we went to check in, we were told all flights had been cancelled. There had been an airplane accident at the airport in Chicago. I couldn't get out until the morning. Naturally, I arrived in Chicago late, the classes had already begun, and Jimmy had already made a name for himself— he was insane, but funny. Instead of going to my room, I had my bags sent up and I went right to class. Walking in, the speaker looked at me and asked.

"Are you Ellie?"

"Yes, I am," I replied. To my astonishment the whole class started applauding. I went and sat next to Tom.

"What the fuck is going on?" I said to Tom.

"What happened, why you didn't come last night?" he asked.

"There was a plane crash. Haven't you seen the news? I said sarcastically.

"No, last night was insane, you'll see, give it time."

Nothing more was said and after the meeting I went to their room. No, I went to their suite and we discussed the classes, they invited me to join them for dinner, but I declined. That afternoon, I had called the office and Cathy told me that Winston had sent me the most beautiful flowers. I asked her to please throw them out. I didn't want to see a thorn, or a leaf when I returned. I just needed to get some sleep; it had been a crazy couple of days. I ordered room service, took a bath but did not shave my legs. I just wanted to relax. When I came out of the bathroom I went over the material from the class that day and fell asleep. I had no idea what time it was, but my phone was ringing and it was Jimmy, drunk and totally out control.

"Ellie, it's me."

"Yes, Jimmy. I know it's you," I answered him.

"I can't sleep, I can't sleep without my wife," he told me.

Then he started talking about his wife and how much he loves and misses her. He asked me if I could talk dirty to him so he could go to sleep.

"No, I am not going to talk dirty to you. I don't do that I wouldn't even know what to say."

"I'll tell what to say and then you can just repeat it back to me," he said, I couldn't believe it.

"No, I am not doing that either."

"Ellie, if you don't I'll just keep calling you all night long".

"Jimmy please go to sleep. I'm tired, and haven't slept in I don't know how long. I have to go to sleep now, as I am really tired," I was getting annoyed.

"Can I come to your room? What's your room number?" he insisted.

"I am not giving you my room number. I'll stay on the phone with you until you fall asleep, but if you say anything sexual I will hang up this phone."

He finally agreed and then started talking about how much I impressed him in that meeting with Richard. He told me how upset Tom was when Richard wanted to fire me.

"You know my cousin is in love with you," he said, "I know you are in love with him," he was rambling.

"I am not in love Tom and he is not in love with me, we have a special relationship, we are really good friends."

"He's in love with you. If you are not in love with him then give me your room number to prove it!"

"Don't be ridiculous. You are talking such garbage. You don't know what the fuck you are talking about, we are just friends."

But, Jimmy had to take it a step further and he was insane. Any fantasy I could have dreamed about with Tom was nothing to what Jimmy said next.

"Don't tell me you don't dream about Tom, don't tell me that you don't dream about Tom's hands moving slowing across your body and touching every part of you."

"Stop it, Jimmy, Please?"

"Tell me that you wouldn't like it, because you know you would be lying to me. I'm going to hang this phone up and I'm going to find your room," he slurred.

The thought of this lunatic running around the hallways frightened me.

"Okay Jimmy I would like it, is that what you want hear?"

"Yeah!" he answered excitedly, "do you see Tom's face and his lips?"

"Yes, Jimmy I see it," I responded.

"Now imagine him devouring you with every kiss and pressing his body against you?"

He went on and on. Apparently, Jimmy was a professional at phone sex. He was getting crazier. I cannot write down all the things he was saying, he was very good and I still blush today remembering his words.

But, telling me all the things Tom was going to do to me was actually turning me on. I knew it was insane, but I didn't know what to do, he talked all night. I don't know when I fell asleep, but I awoke the next morning with the phone at my ear. I missed my wake up call.

I walked into class one hour late and the speaker stopped speaking.

"Rough night Ellie?"

"Really rough," I responded with a smile, and the class started laughing. Then I looked at Tom and he was mad that I was late. He wrote on piece of paper.

"I tried calling you and your phone was busy, what happened?"

I wrote back, "Jimmy called and I was on the phone with him all night.

"That was YOU he had on the phone?"

Tom wrote back: "Apparently, Jimmy had called half the women in the class. He got the list of all the phone numbers for every one in the seminar."

After listening half asleep to the speaker, at lunchtime Tom and I went to grab a bite to eat. I told him how out of control Jimmy was, but I didn't tell him what Jimmy had said to me. He thanked me for keeping Jimmy on the phone because if I didn't we probably would have been thrown out of the seminar.

A MEMORABLE EVENING

That evening, Jimmy rented out one of the banquet rooms for dinner. He invited over thirty people from the franchise offices throughout the country. Jimmy was paying for all of it. He proposed a toast.

"Let's drink to New Beginnings, New Friendships and Success! I would like to say a few words in front of you all tonight, and that is to have a successful business you need certain components," he began, "First, a company needs an image and for our company that is Tom."

He made Tom stand up and continued.

"Secondly, you need a negotiator, someone who can talk to people and gain their trust in order to close the deal. That person is Richard."

Richard stood up.

"Then you need the man with ideas and the money. That is I!" He took his hand and pointed to himself. He talked about the good combination.

"But, folks, we never truly succeeded until we had Ellie. She is the heart of our company, the one who everyone goes to. She showed me how to respect my employees because like our bodies, a company cannot beat without a heart. So would everyone raise their glass to our heart, to our Ellie," he said, and the crowd applauded.

"To Ellie!" They called.

I couldn't believe Jimmy had said this. I was proud and honored. I had worked so hard all these years and never thought Jimmy even noticed. Well, needless to say I was not left alone. We left the room when the bar closed, and unbeknown to us Jimmy had a case of Champagne delivered to the lobby. I sat at the piano with a female agent from Georgia and watched Tom get plastered.

"Don't tell me you play the piano too?" He asked, and before I had time to respond, Tom yelled out to everyone.

"There's nothing this girl can't do."

"Yes, I can't play piano," I said laughing. The woman I was sitting next to told me to just put my fingers on these keys and play four notes, I did. Tom just stared at me with a grin—a dirty, sneaky, little grin. I didn't know what to do, so fuck it I joined them and drank. My feet were hurting so I removed my shoes. I found one owner from the Oregon office wouldn't leave me alone. I was drunk, but wasn't drunk enough to let that man come back to my room.

"I think that you're a little woozy, Ellie, I won't do anything, I just want to make sure you get back to your room safely," he told me. *Sure,* I thought, *you won't do anything.*

"I'm fine, I just need to find my shoes," I said, putting my hand up to him as a gesture to stop. I looked everywhere for my shoes, crawling on the floor to look under the sofa and I found one. I raised my hand with the shoe proud to have found one, but when I looked up, Tom was standing above me. He was laughing and shaking his head. My newfound friend from Oregon came over wanting to help, but Tom pushed the guy away and told him that he was walking me to my room. Tom looked at me.

"You really are drunk," he laughed.

"I know, I need to go my room, but I can't leave yet, I can't find my shoe."

"Forget the damn shoe, you are going to your room!" he ordered and grabbed my arm pulling me towards the elevator. I knew at that moment Tom had no intentions of anything happening between us, he was truly just taking me to my room.

The problem was my room, when I tried to book the room the hotel was full. I begged them to give me any room.

Remember the television show "Get Smart" where the guy goes through door after door to get to his office. Well, that was my room. I think I was staying in the staff section. First we took the elevator, walked down a corridor, which I could not find at first, then took another elevator down to another floor, and then there were about four different corridors I had to turn.

"This can't be right Ellie, we're lost. We are fucking lost. I don't even know where we are anymore." I assured him that we were going the right way.

"You're drunk and you don't know where you are going," he was angry.

"I know where I am going, follow me," I said, pulling away from him.

It was late and there was no one in the halls to ask directions, but eventually I found it.

"Look, here's my room, I found it."

"Are you sure this is your room?" He asked, and I pulled out the key.

"Here, check the number," I said confidently. I lifted up the key and pointed to the number on the door. He grabbed it from me and opened the door.

"Tomorrow you are switching your room," he told me.

"My room is in the slave quarters, a lot different from your fancy suite," I laughed. We walked into the room; my bed was a mess with all the paperwork and books from the classes. My clothes were just thrown everywhere. Mr. Meticulous was looking at my room and I beat him to it.

"I'm a slob, I am a drunken slob," I muttered, moving the papers off the bed. I threw everything onto the floor, then walked over to him and looked at his face.

"I'm a slob and I don't care."

"I don't care either," he said, grabbing me and kissing me. Everything Jimmy had said to me the night before was coming true. It was perfect, and maybe it was the Champagne. But, was my secret fantasy coming true? I don't know, but I felt like we were one person. Everything was perfect; the way he touched me, kissed me and held me close.

It's been almost thirty years now and if I close my eyes, I can still feel the way he touched me, and how he felt inside of me. Everything was perfect! We made beautiful love and he kissed me again and again.

"I don't ever want to hurt you," he whispered. When those words came of his mouth something happened. Reality came popping back into my brain. *He's married. He's your boss, and he was with a flight attendant two nights ago!* My thoughts screamed inside me. I jumped out bed and stood naked in front of him (which is really shocking because no man had ever seen me naked—not Mark, Winston or Joe) and I was not embarrassed.

"Give me your shirt!" I ordered.

"What?"

"I said give me your shirt."

Tom got out bed and found it on the other side. He handed me the shirt, and I put it on, as I was buttoning the shirt I asked him to give me two dollars.

"What the hell are you doing?"

"I have to get Cocoa Cola. I have to sober up, because what we just did was wrong." He could see that I was upset, and took the money out his pants shaking his head.

"You're fucking nuts!"

"NO! We are fucking nuts, what the hell did we just do? I'll be right back, don't go anywhere."

God knows how I found the vending machine. I was sobering up just walking with all my insecurities coming back. I began talking to myself.

I didn't shower this morning because I was late. I didn't shave my legs, what did I just do? Oh my God!

I walked back in the room and handed him a diet coke.

"It's time to sober up," I said guzzling the can of coke. I don't know exactly what I said, all I know is I was blabbering, saying how wrong it was, that we were friends and he was married. I sat on a chair for a while and then sitting on the bed we talked. The only thing I truly remember is when he said, "It's all Jimmy's fault." And I agreed.

We decided never to be together again. But we were both weak and Tom rationalized the situation we were into it for both our benefits.

"We won't be together again, right?" He pointed out. "You said only one night and this night is not over yet, and this time I want to remember everything," his eyes met mine. He didn't wait for my response, and he grabbed me and pushed me down. He started kissing me and I remember the second time neither of us closed our eyes. We looked in each other eyes with each movement. It was as if we were trying to remember every feeling, every moment, we spoke to each other with our eyes.

Maybe that's why the memory of him has never left me. The second time I wasn't as drunk, and I knew at that moment I was so in love, and had been for years. I don't remember him leaving; he wasn't there when I woke up. Sometimes I think I may have imagined the events of that evening, or maybe it was a combination of what Jimmy had said the night before and what actually happened between Tom and I. All I know is that our lovemaking was different and we became one. It wasn't the alcohol, and I had been with men under the influence before. I felt something that I had never felt before.

I knew it wasn't a dream and wondered how I was going to face him now. Would he see through me and know what I was feeling? But, I couldn't think about that now. I had to get to class, another day without showering. I started to get dressed and remembered that I only had one shoe. I hadn't thought to bring another pair of shoes with me, as I had packed so quickly. I called the front desk to ask housekeeping if they had found my shoe. The only other thing

I had brought was a pair of snow boots, back then you did not wear your snow boots with a suit.

On the third day of class I walked in wearing my grey furry boots, I was most embarrassed. I looked at the speaker's podium and there was my shoe. I walked over and laughed.

"Oh good! You found it," was all I said, picking up the shoe. The speaker went to podium and spoke into the microphone.

"You were right class, it was Ellie's shoe. We had bets going on here. #1 if you were going to be late and #2 that the shoe would be yours."

The entire class was laughing. Talk about the walk of shame. I went and sat next to Jimmy. He told me that Tom was not feeling well and wouldn't be coming to class. Jimmy never said anything to me. I never knew if he was aware of what happened that night. I didn't see Tom for the entire day. I had dinner in my room that night, I finally showered and I had a lot of time to think.

Why did I do that? Why did I think this was a mistake? Why? Why? I beat myself up. Then the other part of my brain told me that it was because he was married, and also my boss. He had even told me on the flight that he had hooked up with a flight attendant and was meeting her at the hotel on Saturday.

He didn't just cheat on his wife with you. He's no different than your father; he's not in love with you. I thought.

MEMORIES

That evening I remembered every moment that we had spent together throughout the years. The morning breakfast we would share, the Gonzales' incident, the way he would walk out of the office to say good morning to me, the time I tried to quit smoking and he bought me a pack of cigarettes.

"Please smoke Ellie, your useless to me this way," he said, smiling at me. Then there was the day in the car when I thought I had cancer. I remembered how he took control, the look on his face when he had to tell me I was being fired. Christmastime decorating the office, the talks, the arguments, and the laughs we had shared. I experienced the happiest moments in my life during these last few years when I was with him.

The confidence he had seen in me, he saw something I never knew was inside of me, but mostly it was the way he looked at me. I remember writing him a letter that night and it was all lies. I don't know what I wrote or even why I wrote it. I know it was to reinforce that this would never happen again.

As women, we have so many insecurities, but the worse thing is feeling like a whore, and that's what I felt like. I'd never been with a married man. I changed this year, had been with two, but I didn't lie to them, they knew about each other. The other reason was all the rumors I heard through the years about Tom and I being involved. This may sound strange, but sleeping with Tom took away my worth, and somehow invalidated my hard work all those years. It made all the rumors valid. I remember when I left Mark, and my father told me that I had chosen my job over my husband. I didn't do it with Mark, but I did do it with Tom. I chose my job over Tom. I had respect at the job, something I never had in my life. I had many people love me, hurt me, and leave me. My job was my independence and security, it allowed me to leave Mark and still take care of my children. That night I felt I made the right decision, not because I didn't love him, but I could lose him by loving him.

The next day there was no class, we were going to the warehouse to pick out office furniture and equipment for the new office. I went in the van with Tom and Jimmy and the place was massive. There were hundreds of square feet of furniture and equipment. The three us were standing listening to the instructions and layout of the warehouse, just as the gentleman was speaking, I looked over and saw this cherry wood modular desk.

"That's absolutely beautiful," I whispered to Tom. He walked with me and I told him that this was perfect. The salesman showed us the reception desk, the conference room table, and the chairs. I saw a fabric that I loved; it came in green, blue and mauve. Then I walked over to the carpet section and picked out the carpet to match the fabric perfectly.

"There, I think that we are finished," I said, looking at Tom.

Jimmy thought I was crazy. There were a thousand things to look at. He objected to my making a decision that fast, he felt that I was being impulsive and wanted us to look around more.

"I like what I like," I said, looking at Tom. He let Jimmy have his way and we spent the next two hours walking around the warehouse. Nothing was as nice as what we had picked out earlier. I had no idea what everything cost and Tom did not tell me.

Jimmy was leaving in the afternoon, I was leaving the following day, and Tom was leaving the day after that. Tom and I went to dinner and we spoke of nothing that happened between us, we were back to business. I went back to my room and cried the whole night hoping he would knock on my door. I could take it all back and tell him the truth, because now I knew the truth.

When he told me that he never wanted to hurt me, I knew he would if we continued. I have never loved anyone the way I loved Tom. I loved him in my soul, I knew him, yes he was moody, he was arrogant, but I loved him. When I saw the bad things about him, I would point them out and he would stop. I never listened to any man the way I listened to Tom. I could be both child and woman, he knew me the same way I knew and respected him.

MEMORIES ARE FOREVER

In thinking about all the relationships I have had in my life and how they hurt me, I often wonder if I had given Tom the chance to love me, and opened up my heart, and then he hurt me, I knew I could have never have survived. So many years have passed since that night and I still torment myself thinking about what may have happened if I had shut my mouth and let him talk. I could have enjoyed the night and seen where it would have taken the two of us. I don't have too many regrets in my lifetime, but this night

I truly regret not because it happened, but what I did afterwards. There is a song by Billy Joel called *"This Night"* I listen to this song and it brings me back to that night. I often wonder if it was the best night of my life or the worst. I've always thought I knew what love was, and at this stage of my life I know the difference between love and sex.

Did you ever have a dream and it came true? Well mine did, and for the first time in my life I was afraid. It's been almost thirty years now, and it was only one night, but I just close my eyes and put on that song and still remember the touch, the kiss, and the tenderness. That night has never left me and never will. It wasn't the sex. It was an orgasmic feeling as one. I know I didn't dream it, but I know I have held on to the dream of what could have been between us. When life turns in a different direction, or when I have heartaches and pain, I always think about Tom and the happiness with him that he never knew. I wrote many times about this night, but I cannot share them with you because they were destroyed. You will read about that in Chapter 15.

Before I left my hotel room, my phone rang and I answered.

"Tom?" she asked.

"No," I said, and the woman hung up. I never asked Tom, but I am pretty sure it was his wife.

I returned home, and my ex-husband (now officially divorced) had been watching the girls while I was away. He was cold and abrupt.

"What the hell is your problem?" I asked and he threw a business card at me, "YOUR BOYFRIEND LEFT THIS FOR YOU," he yelled.

I looked at the card and started laughing.

"Are you kidding, do you think after all these years I would be interested in Julio, give me a little more credit than that," I said, explaining that he was in the hospital. Winston arrived, so to avoid him I spoke with Julio, nothing more. I promised him.

The following day I called Julio, he bullshitted his way around saying he wanted the four us to be together again like the old times. This brought Mark and I closer, we laughed about this and started becoming friends again. He would call up once in awhile and pretend that he was Julio. I would start laughing. I liked him being my friend, and I was tired of being angry with him.

I decided to take the week off that Tom had promised me when I went out to Chicago. Tom had told everyone in the office not to call me that I was on vacation, and whoever did would be fired. My first day back to work Cathy told me that Tom had left his wife.

Oh my God, Oh my God! was all I kept thinking in my head?

Tom's office was now the old conference room, he hadn't arrived that morning and I went to my desk. My mind was racing:

> *"What is he going to say to me?*
> *He loved me and he left his wife?*
> *His wife found out about us and threw him out?*
> *Should I run out of there?*
> *What was I going to do?*
> *What was I going to say to him?"*

When he finally came in, I was on the phone. He knew I was there because my car was parked right in front of the office. He walked straight into his office not even looking at me. When I got off the phone he called me on the intercom.

"Come into my office." He didn't say my name and he always said my name. I was shaking and my mouth was dry, I couldn't even speak. I sat in the chair in front of his desk and Tom went straight to business. At the end he surprised me.

"I have hired Cathy to be my personal secretary. You need not concern yourself with any of my needs, and by the way I did not leave my wife because of you," he said, with no emotion.

I don't know if it was his coldness or the way he glared at me, but I knew I hated him at that moment. I glared back, finally getting my words out.

"I didn't think so," I said in stern voice, and walked out as quickly as I could.

The end of the year came quickly, but no Christmas party, if there was I don't remember one, everything was dark and cold in and out of the office. I now had been off my medication for two months, I had started panicking, thinking that I may be pregnant by a man who hated me and couldn't look at me. If I was pregnant, I was not having his baby. No I can't do that, I could never have an abortion, I love my children, and I would love to have another child.

Okay I thought, if I'm pregnant I would have the baby, but I would move away and he would never know. My mind was racing. I bought a pregnancy test and it was negative, another week went by and still no period. I couldn't take any more, so I called my doctor in a panic.

When I walked in his office he grinned at me and told me there was no need to examine me.

"I know you're not pregnant, your chances are so slim, you are not even off the medication two months and it's still in your system, you must be under a lot of stress. Are you?" he asked.

"You have no idea how much stress I am under," I started laughing. He confirmed I was not pregnant and I was relieved, but another side would have liked it to be God's way of telling me that we were meant to be together. I was a little sad, but relieved because he hated me. I couldn't take the way he looked me. His eyes were daggers now throwing spears at me. When he looked at me I felt little shocks throughout my body. I remember feeling a stinging inside my body. I accepted that it was business, and never looked right into his face for a very long time. That evening I wrote a poem:

My Gentle Man

Where is that gentle man
Don't hide I love him
I saw your lies I heard your truth
I saw your cold I felt your warmth
I saw your fears I know your strengths
Don't turn away don't run away
Please let this gentle man live again
Find this man live your dreams
Be the man you were meant to be
The man who is so special to me

At the end of the year on my 31st birthday, we closed the second office and went to say goodbye to the staff who wouldn't be coming with us. The new office wouldn't be ready till June, but we were starting the franchise out of this office on the first of January. I walked back into my office to my desk. Dr. Joe was standing there next to a beautiful flower arrangement on my desk. Before I could speak, Cathy ran over in front of the flowers to say they were not from Dr. Joe they were from all us.

Cathy knew I was going to throw those flowers right in his face. It had become office policy that if Winston sent flowers, don't tell me about them, just make sure they are thrown out before I came in. Joe started laughing as Cathy threw her body in front of the flowers.

"Happy Birthday," he said, in soft sexy voice, which I had heard too many times before. I looked at him, or should I say, I glared at him.

"Right day. Wrong year." I turned my back and walked out of the office. I could hear everyone.

"Whoa did she let you have it!" they were saying.

"S-she is still m-mad, huh?" Joe stuttered.

"It's too soon Joe," Victoria said, simply.

I always remained close with Vanessa, and all of Marks's family. I never involved them with our problems. Matty was back in my life, he was my friend before Mark, and now he was my friend again. His marriage wasn't going too well, and he would come over to hang out with me. He really liked my poetry. He liked to write poetry also, but he would never let me read it.

Our bond was never broken. He wasn't strong, and when he was upset that was usually when I saw him. I would listen to him; he needed someone to listen. At times I was his sister, his mother, but always his friend. This past Thanksgiving, Matty took the girls and me to the Macy's Day Parade. Danielle and her daughter came with us. Since Thanksgiving he'd been coming around a lot more because he had a crush on Danielle. Back then he couldn't do anything because he was still married. Every time Danielle knew that Matty was coming over, she always found a way to pop in. She did this thing with her eyes, like lift her eyebrows and open her eyes really wide whenever he wasn't watching us.

At that time I thought they would end up together. No more men, I was done! Danielle and Matty would tease me about it all the time. If we were walking outside and a single man walked by he would comment.

"Go for it, let me see whom else you can fuck up."

"Leave me alone, only friends, no more love, no more dreams," I would answer.

He always told me that the right man would either, come into, or come back into my life. I never had any secrets from Matty.

It was the end of another year and what a year. Three men and I had totally fucked up my life. I was done, no more men. I was going to work really hard next year to make the franchise a success.

———

CHAPTER THIRTEEN

THE STORM

It was a new year and I decided to go back into therapy. Elizabeth, my therapist was stumped by my actions and like most she did not give her opinions. We were back to the stage of her listening and me talking.

By February Tom's indifference to me was easing up a little. He didn't glare at me as much, but he was still not talking. Now he was a single man, he acted like a complete jerk. He would talk and laugh about his newest conquests. I remember one day walking into the office, apparently he had been out partying hard the night before, and he looked like shit. He was always beautifully groomed but not this day. His hair was barely combed, he had an open shirt with his chest exposed, and he was giggling like a child while I was trying to go over the business deals. I had finally had it with him.

"You have to stop. I don't care what you do out of this office. But you can't come to work like this." I was really mad and he never said a word. "You need to set an example for everyone here, figure out if you want this? If you don't then we can both walk away now, before any more money is invested." I said sternly, looking right into his eyes.

He quickly apologized and told me that I was right and he would never come into the office looking that way again. I thanked him and walked out, but then I walked right back in.

"Could please just button up your shirt?" he started laughing, put his head down and began buttoning his shirt and tucking it into his pants. I walked out shaking my head smiling, he was such a child, and I was so glad to see it. I felt he was like me after being tied down to a marriage that was suffocating. He needed to find himself and learn to live again, to feel peace and freedom.

OH, WHAT A NIGHT

One Tuesday evening, we were attending the last sales seminar for the Florida homes. Winston showed up in his khaki pants, looking like Winston. To my surprise Victoria yelled at him.

"You are a moron the way you show up. Do you think the way you look Ellie would ever want to take you back?" Victoria pulled no punches. "Look at her, she's a business woman respected by every man in this room. You show her disrespect looking the way you do. You are never going to get her back."

I was uncomfortable from the moment I saw Winston. I was standing against the wall looking at him and then at Tom. In my mind why couldn't it be Tom who was crazy about me and not Winston? Why couldn't I be honest with Tom, what was wrong with me? What am I protecting? Was it my pride, I didn't know? Everyone was making plans to go out afterwards, but I told Tom that I wouldn't go if Winston came with us.

"No problem, Winston is out!" he exclaimed.

We went to a few clubs in Manhattan. I don't know why but I had to drink, it was the last bar we went into. I like to go downtown and we were all feeling pretty good. Victoria and I sat in a booth and two gentlemen approached our table. One gentleman was about to sit next me and suddenly Tom came striding over.

"I don't like your tie," he told the guy right out of the blue. Tom was not a fighter, but he just said what someone would say to provoke a fight. I quickly apologized to the man and got up and put my hand on the lapels of Tom's jacket.

"Stop this, you are not going fight a man because you don't like his tie," I said laughing, "Let's go Tom." I suggested.

"No," he said, "dance with me, you've never danced with me."

"Fine, we will dance."

It wasn't a slow dance. I think that would have been better. I don't know what we were doing; the salsa, the rumba the hustle, the music was fast and sensual. I knew every move he was going to make and he was glaring at me and coming up with moves. I had no idea how I knew how to do them. Everyone stopped dancing and they were watching us.

At the end of the dance, Tom swooped me up into his arms.

"There!" was all he said, and walked away. I overheard L.P. say to Tom there was no way that was the first time we had danced together.

"With Ellie you only get one time," he said, loud enough for me to hear. He looked over and held his drink up to me.

"Right?" he signaled.

He was drunk and I didn't know what this meant (or maybe I did). I was the designated driver that night as usual, but this night I drank. I remember driving on the West Side Highway where they had construction going on. Before I realized it I was on the wrong side of the road, dodging the oncoming cars. I was petrified, but every one else in the car thought it was like being on a roller coaster. I weaved in and out of the oncoming cars.

They were screaming, "Wow! Whoa! Wahoo!"

Everyone thought this was fantastic, I was scared shitless, the tunnel was coming up and there was no way for me to cross with the concrete barriers. Finally, I saw the rubber tubes sticking up dividing the lanes at the entrance to the tunnel, I pulled the car over the tubes not caring if another car was coming and made it to the tunnel in the correct lane. They were all cheering.

"We knew you could do it! We knew you wouldn't let us die!" They all sang out.

"That was a lot of fun, can we do it again?" Tom asked.

They were all drunken idiots. I left everyone at their cars and went home. I didn't care how anyone got home that night.

I managed to go to work the next day. Mark and I had planned to go to Atlantic City. The new and improved Mark was around supporting me in everything I said and did. I even told Mark he could move back in, but he wanted to get married again.

"I don't like marriage, if you want to come back and live with us, I'm fine with that," I told him, but he was quick to answer.

"I would only come back if we got married, Ellie!"

He didn't come back and we stayed friends.

We had set a date a couple of weeks before to do something together. When I got home from work, I laid down for a little while then the doorbell rang, it woke me up. I told Mark that I would iron my shirt and we could go.

The old Mark had came back.

He was mad that I wasn't dressed and waiting at the door for him. He said I was just playing games.

"What Mark? What games? You wanted me to go on a date and I accepted. I'm wrong for being tired? I worked all day and last night I had the seminar."

An argument started and he got meaner and meaner.

"I don't love you, I did this because I wanted to hurt you," he yelled.

"Well, at least you told me while being sober; we can't use the excuse that you were drunk. You didn't hurt me tonight, you hurt me too many years ago, now get the fuck out! Get the fuck out!" I roared.

When he left I was not upset. I think Mark knew when I opened the door it was over between us. I think when he looked in my eyes and didn't see the love that was there years earlier. He knew I hadn't forgotten what happened in our marriage. In my mind, I knew how Mark hurt me, and I was hoping he had changed. But tonight, seeing how upset he was, I knew the act he had been playing with me and I would see through it.

Finally this chapter is over. The boy I loved was gone forever. I truly hated the man he had become. That night I wrote this poem:

Rest in Peace
When someone has died and left our side we tearfully cry

Rest in Peace
All whom have loved will share the sorrow
We pray in their sleep
Rest in Peace
It's not just people that die
There are so many things on this earth that die
Some cannot be seen only felt by the heart
When a love dies you can't see that it is gone nor can you
touch its loss
You can only feel its emptiness and sadness
We had a great love for a while
A love filled with warmth passion and honesty
We cannot revive this love or try to reincarnate our love
Our love was special between only us
We both know that this love died many years ago
In time the pain will disappear the lies will leave my ears
So at this time we must put our love to sleep
And finally let our love
Rest in Peace

I was both busy and excited about the new office. Tom ordered all the furniture, and cost was not a factor. The conference room table alone was over 30,000 dollars. On top of that there was the reception area and office stations throughout. Tom worked with the owner of the building on the office layout. I was responsible for decorating and picking out paint colors, wall paper, and phone systems. Tom thought that French doors would look great, stained in cherry to match the other furniture. He felt that the carpet I had picked out was too expensive and he wanted me to pick out another.

He was very hand's on about everything, especially the artwork. I had watercolor paintings that my friend had painted in my office. I suggested having the same artist do watercolors of different homes on Staten Island. Perfect for a real estate company, he loved the idea and hired her. We supplied various pictures of homes we liked for her to paint. It was a great thing that we did.

We ended up with twenty pictures throughout, all of which carried with them a story. The paintings were beautiful, some were historic and others were just beautifully designed homes. Tom and I worked together well and designing the office was a pleasure.

Picking out anything with Winston was horrible. It always turned into a big debate. I'd pick something, he'd pick something else. I was reminded of the same nightmare it was to pick things out with Mark, his mantra was always.

"We don't need it!"

Not arguing and not having to beg or convince was new to me. I saw Tom's vision and he saw mine.

Armani's girlfriend was arriving from overseas. Armani wanted Victoria to go out to dinner with them. Victoria had been suspended from driving and she didn't want to go to dinner alone. She wanted me to ask Tom to go with her. Tom refused, but I begged him and told him I would drive him to Manhattan. Victoria was already in Manhattan taking DWI classes, Tom agreed reluctantly.

I was alone with Tom and something stupid came out of my mouth that day.

"I'm thinking of going back to my husband, Mark." Tom looked at me with disgust

"Are you crazy?" he asked.

"Well, we are talking again, ever since our divorce we have become friends and I do have two children with him," I explained.

"You can't go backwards Ellie, especially to someone who hurt you so badly," Tom reminded me.

I suspect I said what I did to fulfill my dream that Tom would want me and love me. Maybe I thought that if Tom knew Mark was back in my life, he would declare his love for me.

Ellie, who are you kidding? You couldn't go back after what we shared together, but maybe I could get my friend back who I missed so desperately. I had no intentions of going back with Mark it was over.

I dropped Tom off at the restaurant, and he begged me to go inside with him. I wasn't dressed to go to dinner, but when the dinner was over I told him that I would pick both of them up. They were so drunk when I went back to get them, they crawled in to the back seat and acted like two children. I felt like a mother with two bad kids in the back.

After that Victoria and Tom became good friends and it bothered me. Victoria had no idea about what happened between us. I still wasn't sure if anything really had happened. I made more out it then I should have.

We had a convention in Miami in May, only a few weeks before our official move. Victoria, Brian, Dennis, Tom, Jimmy, Richard and I were all attending. Victoria and I left a few days earlier and drove to Miami. I stayed at my sister's condo in Pompano Beach and Victoria was at her parents place with her cousin Terry.

The first day of classes was a round table discussion for owners and managers. I was surprised when Tom didn't show up. I was the only agency without an owner present. As it turned out Tom had been partying all day with some young girl he had picked up. We had plans with our sales agents that evening to have dinner. I was angry with Tom for acting like a child. I seemed to be the only one who cared about the convention being successful. I remember walking with the sale agents to the restaurant and he began teasing me about my seriousness. I took offense to that.

"I don't care what you do at night, but you could at least go to the classes," I screamed at him.

TOM SHOWS HIS COLORS

That night everyone wanted to party, we decided to go out to one of the many clubs in Miami. In retrospect, I should have stayed home. We were enjoying ourselves, when a cute guy asked me to dance. I didn't get a chance to respond because Tom chased him away. Victoria got on his case and told him it was not the right thing to do, they argued and then went off to dance leaving me standing all alone. I didn't want to dance and wanted to go back to the hotel. I had a lot of classes the next day, but of course when I told them we should go, they teased me as being a party pooper. I decided to take cab back to the hotel and I left.

The next morning I realized Victoria did not come home, we were sharing a room together. I felt angry about my suspicions. After going to class I found that Tom and Victoria were nowhere to be found. It was a long day for me and hard to pay attention. I returned at 5 p.m. and as the elevator stopped on one of the floors, Tom and Victoria walked in laughing hysterically, they apparently were drunk and Tom had a bottle of Champagne in his hand.

They both looked at me and started laughing.

"Whoops!" Tom said when he saw my face. I looked at him and the blood rushed to my head.

"How could you do this to me?" I exploded. I fell apart right there in the elevator.

"I hate you and I quit. I'm done!" I screamed.

I got off on the next floor and ran down the staircase crying, I was hysterical. I kept running and found myself at the Marina. I hid on the side of a boat and sat there crying.

How could he have done this with Victoria? He has humiliated me; everything I ever thought must have been a figment of my imagination.

I remember hitting myself in the head saying over and over.

You stupid girl, you stupid dreamer, he was no different than anyone else, you were only another conquest, another challenge, another notch his belt.

I couldn't go back to my room because I didn't want to face Victoria. I stayed at the Marina for over three hours and it was beginning to get dark. I knew I couldn't stay at the Marina. I was in Miami and didn't have a lot of options; I had to go back to my room. I only hoped that Victoria wouldn't be there.

I was relieved to find that Victoria was not there and I started packing. I couldn't blame her, she didn't know about Tom and me. As I walked into the bathroom to get my toiletries, I heard the door open and Victoria walked in.

"Where the hell have you been, everyone has been looking for you? What are you doing?" she demanded.

"Getting the fuck out here, I cannot stay here," I answered.

"What the fuck is going on, Tom is in a panic!" Victoria screamed at me.

"Fuck Tom and fuck you!"

"What is wrong with you?" Victoria was confused.

I raced around the room packing my suitcase and she continued to demand answers. My tears just would not stop.

"Please tell me what's going on, this can't be because we didn't show up for the classes?" Victoria pleaded.

"The classes? I sat in the classes for his company. To make it successful and all he cares about is getting laid," I rambled. "Remember years ago, when his wife called me a wimp? Well, I am a wimp. She called it so many years ago, and I haven't changed. I am still that same loser, no matter what I do in my life I fuck it up. I never see people for who they really are. I see the fantasy I make up in my mind. I fucking hate myself, and I fucking hate him." I wasn't making sense to Victoria, but all the pain was spilling out of me.

Victoria was really nervous.

"You can't drive like this, it's dark, and you don't where you are going. Please wait until the morning? P-please wait? At least calm down before you leave?" she begged.

"I can't . . . I can't . . . I can't breathe!" I started walking towards the door. "I have to get out of here. Now!"

Victoria screamed and ran in front of me to block the door. She stood with her arms spread over the door, facing me.

"I am not letting you out of this room until you tell me what the fuck is going on," she demanded.

I remember staring at her for a moment and then I threw my suitcase down.

"You want to know? You really want to know? I slept with Tom in Chicago and I am in love with him, and probably always have been. I am nothing but a fucking fool," I began to sob.

Victoria hit her head with hands.

"I am so sorry. I would have never slept with him if I had known."

"No Victoria, this is not your fault," I began, "that man slept with you for a reason. I saw him in the elevator and he was spiteful and vindictive. It's not your fault, I am not blaming you, I'm just sorry that you are in the middle of this. Do you understand why I have to get out here? I think I may kill him. I don't want to go to jail. I don't want my children to have to visit me in jail . . . I want to kill that mother fucker." I said, with rage. Victoria started joking.

"You can't kill him. I don't want to lose my friend, and I'll feel responsible. I'll have to raise your kids, go visit you in jail every week, and send you cigarettes," she laughed, but her humor calmed me down.

I finally told her everything that happened with Tom, and how it was destroying me month after month being in the office with him. The only thing I had was this business being successful. If it wasn't, then I had done all this for nothing. She persuaded me to wash my face and calm down. I agreed and went into bathroom. I heard the phone ring and overheard what Victoria was saying.

"Don't come here Tom, whatever you think you could do to make this better you can't. I'm begging you please don't come here," I walked out of the bathroom as she hung the phone.

"He's not going to come here, please stay until the morning?"

"I can't Victoria, I have to go. I'm going to my sister's place. I need to be by myself for little while," I told her, we hugged and then I left.

———————

After the convention was over, Victoria came to my sister's place, and took me out that night. She suggested that the next day we go to the beach. We were on the beach for a little while when I saw Tom standing there. Victoria immediately spoke up.

"I asked him to come here because you both needed to talk before we go back home. Please Ellie, talk with him, he is so upset," she said. He looked at me.

"Can we talk?" Tom pleaded.

He sat down beside me in the sand. I didn't give him a chance to talk. I quickly blurted it all out. I told him of my love for him, and that maybe I had always loved him, I just wasn't sure. I felt that he didn't love me, because he had never said anything, he always just listened. He never said anything regarding us personally, but had always said he needed me in the business. He reminded me that we had made a commitment and he did not want me to leave.

I don't know why, but I agreed to stay.

We returned home and everything moved so quickly getting ready for the move. We went out one more night, and I got really drunk. Tom drove me home, I remember when he was driving I asked him the question that had always bothered me.

"You never ever told me how you felt about me."

The problem was I remembered asking that question, but to this day I don't know what his response was, I have no memory. I assume he said he didn't love me, and I guess I blocked it out. This has haunted me for years. After that night I didn't have another drink for over fifteen years.

The following evening I wrote this poem:

The Ocean of Despair

As we sail through this ocean of our life
Many times we find ourselves at the ocean of despair
What lies ahead is mainly worry and fear
The water of life at times seems so smooth and calm
But we know this is only for a time before we are at this
ocean of despair
Choose your course now if you dare
Or wait for the waves to take you without a care
We have sailed this ocean before but to no avail
We find ourselves again at the ocean of despair
We rode the waves and swam the currents
Then sometimes just drifting going neither here nor there
One thing is certain for sure if not sooner or later
I will return once again to this ocean of despair

CHAPTER FOURTEEN

---❦---

THE AFTERMATH

The new office was ready and the rent had to be paid. I remember the day we moved out of the office, the movers had everything packed and I was standing in my empty office when I heard.

"The movers are waiting for you," Tom yelled.

"I'll be right there, I forgot something," I answered.

I just looked around and saw glimpses of the happy times shared by all of us. I walked over to the wall where my desk had been by the window. I moved my hand across the window where I used to look at Tom.

"Goodbye my friend," I said out loud.

I knew this was the end for Tom and me. I rushed outside showing my excitement for our new office, but I was dying inside.

Memorial Day weekend the office furniture arrived. Tom was nowhere around, there were a few problems with desk measurements, and as usual I worked like a dog. I couldn't do this alone any more! On Monday I put my resignation letter on Tom's desk.

This particular day Tom was mean, he called over the intercom.

"Ellie, could you come into my office?"

He was sitting behind his desk, holding my resignation letter in his hand.

"You made a commitment and you are not leaving." He picked up another piece of paper. "Do you remember signing this? It's your contract and you have to give me two months notice or I will sue you? I don't want it to be this way, but you have forced my hand. We have worked too hard for you just to walk away. I need you to see this through."

Danielle and I had a plan to move to Pennsylvania for the summer to see if we could get jobs up there. The girls would be out of school for the summer and neither of us had anything on the horizon. We thought it would be a good time to test it out. I planned on getting a night shift job, and she would work the day shift at a hotel.

Well Tom, you just fucked me again. I couldn't go anywhere for two months and that would take me to August, and it would be too close to when girls have to go back to school. I just looked at him with utter defeat.

"Fine, you win! But, if I am going to stay here you have to do more. I cannot keep doing this alone. He agreed, and then to my surprise, he picked up another envelope and basically threw it at me.

"Here, you make it so difficult for people to do nice things for you."

I looked in the envelope and inside was Billy Ocean tickets. I loved Billy Ocean. Here I was alone, with tickets to a concert, and if he weren't so mean to me I would have asked him to come with me. Instead, I asked my brother Mikie to go. Here was another low point of my life to remember.

A few weeks later I had found out that Danny's brother, Pat, had passed. I immediately called him. We had not seen each other for at least ten years. I drove to Manhattan and met his wife; she was really pretty and very nice. Danny had told her about our friendship and she was excited to meet me. They had a daughter together. I had never met a woman who wasn't jealous, but I was about too. I had invited her to go with us.

"No, the two of you need time alone," she said, honestly.

I was so surprised that she got it. She knew Danny and I had a true friendship.

We went to Brooklyn Heights. We transformed ourselves back into kids that night walking curbs, sitting and talking on the stoop, catching up with each other's lives. He told me how he had beat heroin, and all about the family problems with his brothers and sisters. He cried to me over losing his brother, he needed his friend, and so did I.

One week later, he disappointed me. He called to ask me to lie for him. He wanted me to tell his wife that I had borrowed money from him. I couldn't lie, he had told me that he was clean and off heroin. I told that him if he was back on drugs, I couldn't keep our friendship. That was the last time I spoke to him. Through the years I tried to get in touch with him, but he went missing. Finally, in 2008 I was told that he had died.

The office was coming together. Everything was how I saw it so many months before in that warehouse. It was elegant. Tom remarked how beautiful everything was, except for the carpet. He looked at me and reminded me about his apprehension about the carpet. We agreed that it was still a beautiful office.

Tom must have looked at those paintings a hundred times, he loved them, he was so proud of his office. Everyone praised me and people began coming back slowly from the past, but it was not the same. Jimmy was released from the nut house, and he was heavily medicated with no life in him. Richard was more like a babysitter now to Jimmy. My office was located in front, and Tom put his office as far away from me as he could. Cathy was now his personal secretary, her office was near mine and she would come in everyday to ask for help. Then one day I just snapped at her.

"I don't work for Tom, you do. So if you don't understand something, go to him you're his secretary, I have other work I have to do."

My office was the only smoking office, because the new office was a non-smoking environment. Tom had filters put into my office. Most of the staff smoked back then, even Tom. My office soon became the smoking office.

We were getting ready for our Grand Opening party. It was July, one year before I went on vacation with Winston at St John's, what a difference a year makes. I was told that Joe was getting married. Winston popped into the office, and I remember Tom giving him the grand tour. When they walked into my office, Tom pointed to the painting on my wall and told him that the same artist had painted all the artwork. Winston looked at the painting and began rambling about how different colors should have been used. Tom knew, by the look on my face, I was about to say something.

"Personally, I like the painting, Winston. I didn't paint the fucking painting. I don't give a shit about coloring mistakes, or whatever the fuck you think. Please just get out here," I told him.

Tom chuckled. Winston never came back to my office.

JOE COMES BACK INTO MY LIFE

A week later I was in my office talking on the phone with Lorraine, we hadn't spoken for over six months. Sophia called over the intercom.

"Joe is here," announced Sophia. *Did she say Joe?* I thought.

"Don't hang up this phone," Lorraine said. "Just put me on speaker and I'll be quiet as a mouse," I told her, "he won't come in here, he's getting married," I said and she was shocked.

"Boy he doesn't waste anytime does he?"

I heard him walk pass my office. I was so relieved because I truly looked like shit. I had permed my hair and it was horrible. I heard him talking to Richard and then Joe, there he was, my kryptonite. I left the phone on speaker as he walked into my office.

"The office is beautiful. Richard told me you designed everything," Joe gushed.

"Yes," I responded. He walked over to the window.

"You have a nice view."

"Yes."

"How have you been?"

"Just fine, thank you."

"How are the girls?" he asked, and walked over to my desk where I had the most recent pictures of the girls.

"They are doing well, getting bigger every year." I answered, "I believe congratulations are in order, I hear that you are getting married."

"Yes, I am," he said, and began walking out. "It should have been you."

I could hear Lorraine on the phone and I immediately took the phone off speaker.

"What the fuck did that mean?" I asked Lorraine. "It should have been me? I don't believe it?" I was dumbfounded. "Lorraine, I hate this fucking man!" I said.

After he had left Victoria, Sophia, and Cathy came into my office, Lorraine was still on speaker. They all told me that he still loves me.

"He is getting married. Did you all not hear that?" I asked.

Richard came into my office and he even thought that Joe still loved me.

"If that is the case," I questioned, "why is he getting married?"

"Because you broke him Ellie, he loved you." Richard told me, "he doesn't love this girl, and it's not too late. If you have any feelings for him you have to let him know before he goes through with it." Everyone agreed.

Richard came up with a plan. He advised me to think it over and he would have Joe come here on Friday. If I cared about him, then I should tell him. It seemed that everything I did with this man had a deadline. Should I keep my mouth shut and just let him get married? Fuck, I truly didn't know what to do.

Victoria, being the only one who knew about Tom, made me see that Tom was just a fantasy, but Joe was real. Yes, we hurt each other, but there was still something there inside me. I had Richard set up the meeting for 10:00 a.m. Friday. Everyone was there to see what was going to happen. I was running late and so was Joe.

When I walked into the office they asked what happened, and I told them that I was running late. Richard and Victoria had imagined the two of us meeting in the parking lot and running away together. I shook my head laughing at them.

"That's not going to happen," Everyone was talking and then the elevator beeped. They all ran in different directions. Sophia couldn't go anywhere she was stuck at the reception desk. Joe saw me and smiled, then walked over to Sophia's desk.

"Is Richard in?" he asked. Richard came walking out of the conference room.

"Good morning, Dr. Joe!" Richard said, and looked at me and nodded. He walked both of us towards my office, and when we arrived Richard announced.

"I think the two of you need to talk," he pushed us both into the office and closed the door.

"What is going on here," Joe asked.

"I have one question," I began, "why did you say the other day that it should have been me that you were marrying?"

"Because I love you!"

"You are marrying someone in three weeks and you stand here telling me that you love me, are you insane?" I asked.

He looked at me, walked over and took me in his arms.

"I love you, Ellie. I never stopped. I can't stop and I don't want to stop!"

"But, you are getting married?"

"I won't get married if you tell me that you love me," he said, and began kissing me.

Here we go again. The smell of his cologne got me every time. I gained my control and pointed to the chair opposite my desk.

"Y-you s-sit over there and I will sit here. W-we should talk."

I knew the minute he held me in his arms, and smelled him again, I was done.

"If you felt this way, why did you wait so long?"

"I came to your office on your birthday. You hated me, I saw it in your eyes."

I explained that my birthday was a bad choice, given he had stood me up the year before.

"Did you really think I would be nice to you," I asked.

"Richard had told me that you ended things with Winston, and I didn't want you to be alone on your birthday, but you didn't even give me a chance to speak," he explained.

"How long have you known this girl?"

I was dating her because I was told that you were with Winston. We met a month after we broke up." He looked at me with a lovely expression on his face. I had forgotten his softness because I was too consumed with hurt.

"You love me," he said, "I know you do, because Ellie you wouldn't be sitting here with me, you would have thrown me out of the office by now," he laughed, and it sounded good.

"I don't know what I feel, Joe. I've been through a lot this past year. I have always cared about you, but you always hurt me and then I do bad things to you."

"Just get married, this is a bad idea, we don't work. I don't even know if this is love, I don't even know what love is anymore?" I sounded defeated.

"I know, we can trigger each other, but that happens when you love someone," he said sincerely. Then he got up from the chair and came around the desk and started kissing me.

"I know Winston never kissed you like me, and I know that Karen doesn't make me feel inside the way you do," he said, looking right into my eyes.

"Joe, b-but this is crazy!" I protested.

"You love me, tell me you love me?" He started kissing my neck. "Ellie, tell me that you love me," he kept insisting.

I waved my hands in defeat.

"You son of bitch, I guess I still do love you," I smiled, lovingly.

He told me that he would take care of everything. He was like a little boy and he promised that everything was going to work out fine this time.

Yes, I got back together with a man who one minute ago had told me he was planning to marry someone else. What else could you expect of my crazy, wonderful incredible life? But there was more to come. Joe called me at home that night, and said he needed to talk with me.

I listened carefully and got sucked in once again. He had a way of doing that to me, and I had left myself wide open again. Here is the bullshit he shoveled onto me. Believe it or not, this guy was good and I must have been blind.

"Ellie, I told Karen that I was in love with you. It broke her heart and she begged me not to embarrass her, she wants me to go through with the wedding, and then we would divorce afterwards. I feel that it is the least I can do for hurting her."

It made sense to me at the time. But, now I know he is a lying bastard. Richard wanted me to be his guest at Joe's wedding. Thank God Joy was going to camp the day of the wedding, and I would be many miles away.

My only relief was to write poems. I called this one:

July All the Away

This July came in with soaring heat and violent summer storms
In the midst of all this
My love returned with all the passion and heat of July
Here we were again in the midst of our summer storm
We have a love that burns stronger that any July sun
The passion between us was thicker than the night's air
Yet our love is more turbulent than any storm imaginable
When I hear thunder it yells at me for my foolishness
When the rain fall it's my heart crying
But when I saw him again the storm ended within me
The sun appeared and so did his heart
With him I feel a sort of peace and happiness
A never-ending passion for love
But in every year July must end

A new month will come

Then again I must say goodbye to my July love.

GRAND OPENING PARTY

Joe got married and called me every day. I thought our relationship was strange in the past, now it was totally a new insanity. I was having an affair with a married man. I think I have broken every single rule when it comes to Joe.

The night of the Grand Opening party the place was packed. Winston showed up wearing one of the suits. He looked very handsome, but he was still Winston. Then by total surprise Joe came over to me.

"I'm not staying. I just wanted to wish you good luck, and if you could do me one favor come downstairs for a moment?" he requested, and I followed.

He opened the car door and asked me to get in. He started the car and put in a cassette tape. The song "All the Way" was playing. I had once told him that I loved that song. I couldn't believe that he found it. As I was listening to the song, he saw me smile.

"I'm singing that, that's me singing," he said, proudly.

I couldn't believe it was his voice it was so beautiful. After we listened to the song he told me to go back to the party. He held me first.

"I love you. I promise to love you all the way," he said, and kissed me goodbye.

The evening was wonderful and a true success. Tom thanked me for everything

"Every one came tonight because of you," he said.

When Tom said those words I knew I had changed. The old Ellie would be ecstatic to hear such kind words from Tom. I thanked him, but remained numb. I didn't have feelings either way towards him. I didn't hate him. I just no longer loved him. It's difficult to love someone if they can't love you back. I thought about Joe, and wondered why he had picked tonight to play me that song.

A few weeks later Tom told me that his mother might have cancer. Then his father called me. He wanted me to tell Tom the results. It was hardest thing I ever had to do, to tell him his mom had cancer. He cried and ran out the door.

THERAPY WITH ELIZABETH

Yes, I was in therapy with Elizabeth. She told me that Joe was not the person for me and I needed to end it. That was the first time I didn't listen to her. We did talk about Tom, but she couldn't help me with him. She felt I had to get away from both of them. She wanted me to leave my job and start over, anywhere.

One month turned into two, the third month rolled around, and Joe was still married. I never see Tom these days, I hear that he's dating a woman name Ava, and he is in love. I know I can't stay at my job any longer. Joe had come over the night before complaining that his wife won't leave the house. We made love that night and then afterwards I gave him an ultimatum

"No more Joe, no more. I can't do this any longer. When you're divorced, if I am here, we will be together, but I am done." He knew that I was serious.

I listened to Elizabeth. I put in my resignation and gave it to Tom. This time he accepted it. I hired my replacement and had a little money saved. I would try to do what I wanted in June. I was going to look for another job in the New Year. I was leaving at the end of the year. I knew I had to get away from the both of them. Joe still called me every day, but I wouldn't see him. He knew I was leaving my job and wanted to see me.

One night he showed up at my apartment without calling, which he never did, because I wouldn't have him around the girls again unless we were together. He came in and told me how much he missed me. He wanted me to promise that I wouldn't move away. I still don't remember why, but as he was talking to me, I remembered that I hadn't gotten my period. I quickly went over the calendar where I always mark an X when I get it. There was no X for November. I put my hand to my head and looked at him.

"I think I'm pregnant!"

"No, not possible. I have a slow sperm count, you can't be pregnant," he said, nervously, "It's just stress and you are under a lot of stress."

I remembered last year the same thing happened around the same time.

"You are probably right, but I am going to buy a pregnancy test tomorrow, just to make sure," I told him.

The very next morning I bought my pregnancy test on my way to work. Sophia came with me into the bathroom. I peed on the stick. She was trying to read the directions out loud, but before she finished I had already slid down the wall with my hand covering my head holding the stick in my hand.

"Calm down, you don't even know yet," Sophia tried to comfort me. Then I showed her the stick with the darkest colored X.

I started to cry and Sophia cried with me. I had given up my job, and my replacement was already in Chicago. Then there was a knock on the bathroom door.

"Who is there?" I asked.

"It's Victoria, let me in?" Sophia opened the door.

"Tom sent me in, he thought he heard you crying, what's going on?" Victoria asked. Sophia showed Victoria the stick.

"Oh my God. Oh my God!" Victoria put her hands over her mouth. "What the fuck are you going to do, I thought you couldn't get pregnant?"

"I thought so too," I responded tearfully.

"Let's sue your doctor. If he didn't tell you that, you would have used protection, right?" We all burst out laughing after she said that. Sophia would always look for the silver lining.

"You got to get out of here and clean yourself up," Victoria told me, "go into your office, Tom is wondering what's going on. I'm just going to tell him that you have the flu."

I went in my office and sat at my desk. I stared at the watercolor on the wall, thinking if I had only left when I wanted to, I never would have seen Joe again.

Tom came into my office holding a cup of tea in his hand.

"Here drink this and calm down," he said. I hadn't seen that side of Tom in a long time. He had concern all over in his face. I was still crying, and I had my arms above my head with my hands covering my eyes. I took a deep breath and removed my hands and looked at Tom.

"Tell me what is going on, Ellie?" I shook my head.

"I can't. I can't," I repeated.

"I'm not kidding, tell me what is going on?" he asked, raising his voice.

"I'm pregnant!" I blurted. I don't think those were words he expected me to say. He was shocked and disappointed.

"And the man is married?" he stated, in a typical Tom fashion.

"Don't have it, get an abortion." I looked at him in shock, "I know, you could never do that," he was resolved and didn't push that issue again. He did ask me if I wanted my job back.

"No, it's not fair to the woman we hired. She is away at this very moment training for my job."

He stayed talking to me for about thirty minutes and told me that he would be there for me if I ever needed him. I wondered how he could be there for me when someone or something else caused me pain. Why hadn't he seen all the months of pain I was in with him? Why did the old Tom have to come back now? It was easier to leave when he was mean to me.

Tom stayed with me until he knew I was all right. As he was leaving he commented.

"Do I know the person?" I nodded my head, yes.

"Dr. Joe?" Tom guessed. I told him yes and then he left.

After he left I sat there even more confused. It took me getting pregnant to get my friend back. I missed my friend, and I did feel better just knowing that he cared again.

Joe called shortly afterward. I told Sophia to tell him that I was on the phone. I wasn't ready to talk with him. I didn't know what I was going to say. I waited about an hour before calling. He picked up the phone.

"Well, are you pregnant?"

"Nope," I said, because I knew exactly what Joe was going to do.

"Ah-ah, there was a part of me that really wanted you to be pregnant, we would have our own baby. We could have a little Joey running around. I'm a little sad, I really wish you were pregnant."

He had said enough for my ears to hear.

"Really Joe, you really want us to have a child together?"

"I really do, I love you."

"Well I lied to you. I am pregnant. Now what do you have to say?"

There was utter silence.

"That's what I thought," and I hung up the phone.

He even tried to bullshit me again. I wouldn't see him and I wouldn't talk with him. I knew I was keeping the baby, I just didn't know what I was going to do. How do I get a job now that I am pregnant? Who would watch the baby after it was born? The first people I told in my family were my kids, Joy and Dawn. We were lying on the bed together. I told them that I had something very important to tell them.

"I am having a baby and Joe is the father," I began. "I don't know if I'm going to marry him, but you are going to have a brother or a sister," I smiled, happily.

Dawn was ecstatic, touching my stomach. I loved Joy's response.

"Can we keep the baby and not Joe?" she asked.

"That's a possibility, we will have to wait and see," I smiled.

I told my parents that I was pregnant, but didn't know if Joe was going be in my life. My mother, in her usual way, put me down telling me that I was a disgusting person to have children from different fathers. She told me that I had to marry Joe, because if I didn't, I would just be nothing but a cheap slut to everyone.

Thank you for your support mom! I truly did not expect her to say anything different, but I no longer cared what she thought anymore. My eyes were open to her, and she couldn't hurt me. My sister had two children with a man she never married, and not once did she say those words to her.

Our Christmas party was my last day as manager at the real estate company. I gave Tom a poem that I had written, printed and framed. It was called, "My Tree of Life. Tom read it aloud to everyone at the table.

My Tree of Life

We all look at many of nature's gifts
Have you ever looked at this tree and seen yourself
The tree just as me lives as we do
In the beginning only roots from its ancestors
As the tree grows a foundation is formed
The tree just as we must branch out to new beginnings
With every branch grows a new experience occurs
With each branch leaves and flower bloom
The tree grows tall wise and beautiful
Now I too must branch out but never to forget
That out friendship is truly rooted
As in the tree we branch out to new beginnings
In these years we grew tall wise and beautiful
In many ways we gained strength from each other
Just as in the tree
A person must grow and leave behind friends and memories
Special friends never to be forgotten
The memories the experiences are now a part of me
Only true friends can see growth as happiness
I consider you a very special branch
In my tree of life
After he finished reading it he hugged me.

"Ellie, I know you wrote it, because it was signed anonymous," Tom said, softly.

I shook my head, yes.

During the party we reminisced about all the fun times and the crazy happenings through the years. It was great!

It was hard saying goodbye to everyone and truly sad saying goodbye to my friend. Everything I feared that day had come true. I left a life that I truly loved. The song from *Dirty Dancing* came to my mind. I sang it to myself on my drive home.

I had the time of my Life!

Every time I hear that song, I think of these days. I owe them all to him.

———————————

CHAPTER FIFTEEN

VIVIFIED

D anielle had come with me to my first doctor's appointment. It was a funny day. My doctor was in awe of Danielle and was talking to her and not me. At one point, here I am lying with my feet in the stirrups and he's actually flirting with her.

"Excuse me, I hate to interrupt the two of you, but . . . " I said, looking at my legs sprawled wide open.

The doctor turned his head towards me.

"I'm sorry let's get back to business."

"Yes, let's please?"

"He examined me.

"Yep, you are pregnant!"

"You told me that I couldn't get pregnant!" I said, feeling most annoyed.

"I guess I'm just not that good of a Doctor," he smiled at Danielle. I was eight weeks pregnant. Such a jerk!

I spent my birthday with Matty and Danielle hanging out in my apartment. We were sitting at my kitchen table and I told him that I was pregnant. He looked at Danielle.

"You knew about this, and you didn't tell me?" he asked, what he said had caught Danielle and me off guard. Why would he say this to her? They weren't a couple, they weren't even friends.

"Why should I tell you? Oh, I should just call you up and say, Ellie is pregnant?"

Then two of them started fighting, but I saw that Matty truly cared for her. Then Danielle who was always the comedian made a joke.

"I would have called you, if I was pregnant and the baby was yours," she said doing that thing with her eyes.

"Well, I would hope so," Matty said, he was angry with her and it made no sense. Then he turned to me.

"Well Elle, this is another fine mess you have gotten yourself into young lady."

We all started laughing. We had a great evening together. Matty never judged me, and he only ever supported me.

"Whatever you need Elle, I'm here for you," he told me.

Christmas, my birthday, and New Year's had come and gone. No Joe. He was truly on a roll, three birthdays in a row.

Once I got home I wrote another poem:

Our Child

You don't want our child
How could that be
Our child was a gift of love
A gift given to you and me
It saddens my soul
And it hurts my pride
For you are not the man
I thought you were inside
The moments we spent together
All those dreams we planned
Were all lies and deception
This I understand
Finally, I see who you really are
For now I know I have nothing to fear
My fear was losing your love
A love that never was there

The New Year came and I was unemployed. I had no idea what would be my next move. Joe called and asked if we could talk. He begged me to go out to dinner with him. He took me to a beautiful restaurant in New Jersey, very fancy with private rooms. We were seated in the room and then ordered dinner. He surprised me.

"Will you marry me?" I looked at him and shook my head.

"Joe, you are married. You can't ask me to marry you."

"She is gone, she moved out," he insisted.

"I don't care, I don't want you in my life, I'm done. It's been over six weeks, Christmas and my birthday have passed and nothing from you," I wailed.

"I didn't come to you until I knew she was definitely gone. No more promises that I couldn't keep. I want to be with you, and I want us to start our lives together today." He took hold of my hand. "Let's clean the slate and pretend this is our first date, the way it should have been," he said, "you are glowing, your eyes are so blue, and you look so beautiful. When you are mad, do you know your eyes get even bluer?" I raised my eyebrows and retorted.

"Then they must be really blue now?" I laughed.

"Well, are you glowing or mad?"

"A little of both," I said. "Look Joe, I don't need you in my life, I can take care of myself, but I am not going to have you come in and out of this baby's life as you have done with mine. You weren't a good father to your daughter, and I will never let this child near you, unless you are going to be in all the way," I was direct with him. He knew I meant what I said.

"I want this baby in my life. I want a do over. I want a family, and I am going to prove to you that I will be a good father. I promise I will never hurt you. I'll never cheat on you, please give me another chance, I'm begging you."

He took my hand, his eyes filled up with tears, and he placed my hand over his lips.

"I love you, Ellie, please give me another chance?"

I took my hand away and explained that I would give him another chance, but I would not move into his home. I did not trust him. I would take tonight as our first date and see where it leads. But, if I decided that I didn't want him my life, he would walk away and never be in the baby's life. I would give the baby his last name either way. He agreed.

"I'm going to prove it. You are never going to want me to leave," he said jokingly. We had a wonderful evening and we danced in a private room, everything was beautiful. I just didn't know if it was all too late for us.

Not knowing what to do, I returned to the real estate office as a sales agent. The new manager was in my old office, and I went into a duplex office with another agent. My memories are a little blurred, I don't think I stayed long, and don't even now if I made a sale. Joe was going through bad financial times. The home he purchased was too expensive and he had trouble keeping up with the payments. He filed for divorce, and Karen was asking for half of the home, which she had put no money into. He had bought that house before he was married, but foolishly he put her name on the deed.

I also found something else that Joe did not tell me. He had paid for her to go back to school to become a Physician's Assistant, another person Joe took care of. I think the reason the marriage didn't break up sooner was because she waited until her graduation. She wasn't working or helping him with anything. He kept persuading me to see the house. I wanted him to sell it, and did not want to move to New Jersey. He wouldn't sell it. He kept telling me how the girls would love the house, and how good the schools were. Joy was going into the sixth grade. In Staten Island you are required to go to junior high in the sixth grade. The junior high in my district was not a good school. I just wasn't ready to make that big decision.

Joe came to my next doctor's appointment. When I reached my fourth month, I went for a check up. They gave me my first sonogram, we saw the baby's heartbeat, Joe was beaming and the doctor kept moving to another section on the screen. He then went and measured something on the screen and showed us a big surprise.

"This is the baby," he pointed to an image. "But, do you see this?" He asked, pointing to an area at the top of the screen. It was a larger object.

"Twins?" Joe yelled out.

"No! Ellie, that's your tumor. It's growing with the baby and your body thinks it is having twins. Now, everything is fine, but we have to watch it. I need you to come in every two weeks for a sonogram. I want to keep my eye on it."

I saw Joe's face and he was terrified. The doctor reassured us that it would be fine. Joe acted strong, telling me that everything was going to be fine. That was the day I knew I did love him and needed him in my life. For the next few months everything was great, Joe didn't sleep over, but he came every night before driving home to New Jersey. He and the girls got along great. Joy was still a little resistant to him. She would look at him from the side of her eye, and then give him a little smirk. Joe used to say.

"See, I'm growing on her. She's going to love me one day, you'll see."

Well, Dawn was very happy when Joe walked in every night.

"Hi honey, I'm home," he would say. Dawn would run and hug him. Later she called him "honey", the two of them were a comedy routine. He would sit on the floor and play with her Barbie dolls, anything Dawn wanted to do they did. They would sing and always laugh together. Sometimes, Joy would be nice to him, but she would always get annoyed about something and walk away. She did not trust him, and Joe knew it.

Life was a dream, we would lie on the couch together, and I would have my jazz music playing while reading poetry to him. He would tell me that this was how the rest of our lives would be. At seven months pregnant, the tumor was still growing and it was time to see the doctor again. He examined me and told us that everything was fine. Then he slapped my leg.

"Now we are having a baby!" he said, excitedly.

"Wasn't I always having a baby? What does that mean?" I asked nervously. He explained that the tumor was above the baby, and it could burst causing the baby to suffocate. (The reason I had the ultrasound every two weeks).

"If the tumor burst now, I can take the baby. It is far enough developed for me to deliver the baby early if need be," he told me. I didn't know if I was relieved or more frightened after hearing that.

MY SECRET

Everything was going great. I was moving into his home in June when school was out. The weekend before, we took the girls to the house and they picked out their rooms. Joy was going to have a sleep over party at our new home on her birthday.

On Saturday we were going crib shopping with my Nanny and my mother. I don't know why, but I had slept at my mom's home the night before. I was going to my apartment to pick up Joe. I left my Nanny and my mother waiting in the car. I walked into the apartment, instantly I knew something was wrong by the look on his face. He was angry. Then I saw what he had in his hand. He was holding my journal with all my poems and thoughts.

"You slept with Tom?" he screamed at me. It was something I did not want him to know, for many reasons. The fighter that I am went on the defense and I yelled right back.

"How dare you read that?" I walked over to him and grabbed the journal from his hand. "This is mine, and it's personal," I started crying.

"Is this baby even mine, or have you made a fucking fool out of me?" He screamed, "I'm going to be raising his kid, and I have to read about how perfect his touch was, how you were one and how you danced . . .?" he was rambling, as he read the words that I wrote. I was becoming angrier with him.

"Do you know what I have done for you? All things I have given up?" He accused. That was it, his last statement made me totally lose it.

"I didn't lie! What you gave up for me? What you have put me through for almost four years? Yes, I did sleep with Tom, and yes, I did fall in love with him, but you were not in my life as usual,"

I screamed out of control. "I was not the one who got engaged to someone and then married someone else in the course of our supposed relationship," He wasn't saying a word. He had a shocked look on his face. "When I am with a man I have to feel something for him. You read the pages and you know how he made me feel, so I'm not going to lie. Yes, I did feel it and it was perfect, like we were one. Did I feel a magic that I don't feel with you? Yes, but up until that night Tom never hurt me, the way you did over and over again. Do you really think I would lie to about our baby?"

We were right back where we started it seemed.

"Joe, I didn't know if I truly wanted you to be in my life. But, when I found out I was pregnant, I saw it as a sign from God and maybe we were meant to be together. Do you think if I were carrying Tom's child, I would want you to be the father? Do you think Tom would let you raise his child? I lied to you once, and only once that was about my vacation with Winston. I didn't lie about Tom, it was one night that is all it was."

"But you love him, you wrote about your love for Tom was stronger than any love you had ever felt. Are you saying that you love Tom more than you love me?" he asked seriously.

I started to calm down and spoke in a much calmer voice.

"Yes," I said. He looked like he was going to kill me. I raised my hand, signaling him to stop.

"Joe, you will never understand what Tom gave me, he saw something inside me, as I saw in him. He gave me strength, he made me grow inside as a person, he gave me confidence and security, but most of all he gave his trust. One thing Tom didn't give was his love. You gave me nothing, except passion and heartache. What was I to think? Was this love or lust? It's only been the last three months after four years that you have come back into my life, and I'm starting to trust you. Please understand that is something I *always* had with Tom."

Joe appeared very pensive. I could tell that he just wasn't listening, but rather he was actually hearing what I had to say.

"Let me ask you this. If Tom had told you he loved you, would you be here with me today?" he asked. I didn't answer right away, I remember rubbing my head and telling him.

"How do I know after the fact?" I said, honestly.

"That's not an answer, I want an answer," he demanded. I screamed right back at him.

"I don't know, who knows anything could have happened. He could have told me he loved me. We could have dated, then later he could have cheated on me, and then left me, and then YES you would still be here today. But, if Tom loved me and he was the man I thought he was than NO, you would not be here today."

Joe, we can play the "what if" game all day. This is our life Joe, it is what it is!"

"You have your past and I have mine."

"FINE," he said, and walked towards me pointing his finger in my face.

"You will never see him again, I want you to promise me that right now."

"Nope, I can't keep that promise."

"Why?" he screamed at me, "Why?"

"Because he's my friend and he did nothing wrong. I did nothing wrong, we didn't cheat on you. You were not in my life at that time and if you were, I never would have slept with Tom, and that's the truth, but it happened," I answered calmly.

I no sooner got the words out of my mouth and the doorbell rang. It was my mother. I had forgotten they had been sitting in the car downstairs all this time. I went to answer the door.

"What's going on, is everything okay?" she asked.

"I will be right down, mom," I told her and closed the door.

I walked into the kitchen where Joe was waiting.

"I'm going shopping for the baby's crib, if you still want to be part of our lives, I'm leaving now. It's your choice, you are welcome to come," I managed to smile.

He acted reluctantly, but he came. We drove to New Jersey and Joe was pleasant to every one. I felt like someone had beaten the crap out of me. Nothing could just go well, it seemed there always had to be drama. I had written various poems, which I have quoted in this story. Sadly, Joe threw out everything I had written about Tom, so I have only shared a few. That day probably changed Joe. He was never able to erase from his mind what he had read.

EVERYTHING WAS DIFFERENT

Darlene had a baby shower for me and all my friends were there. At the end of June we moved to New Jersey and it was really exciting and new. All of us were waiting for the baby. I was nine months pregnant, the girls were away on vacation with their father, and I was cleaning the house. I had my Jazz music blasting and Joe walked in.

"Shut off that music," he yelled, I went over to lower the music. "Shut it off I hate that music," he said.

"You told me you loved it."

"Well, I lied."

"Why did you have to lie, why didn't you tell me you didn't like it?" I cried.

"Because if I told you the truth, you wouldn't be with me. I was trying to show you that we had something in common," he confessed.

I was upset and through the years, as we have met new friends, it has become one of the funny stories we tell them.

The girls returned home from vacation and they were putting on a show for us, earlier that day I painted all the shutters on the house and sure enough I went into labor. Joy was afraid and came out screaming.

"Are you gonna' die mommy?"

I tried to calm her down, and both girls came to the hospital with us, they wouldn't stay with anyone, they were too afraid. I had our son, and we named him Brian after my grandfather. When I woke up in the hospital bed there were flowers all around the room, the nurses arranged them while I was sleeping. Beside me on my nightstand was a beautiful bouquet of roses, I reached over to read the card: "Congratulations! All my love Tom." I could have asked the nurse to move them over to the windowsill before Joe came in, but I didn't.

THREE MONTHS LATER

Tom was moving to Florida and I decided to throw a going away party at my house for him. Joe and I weren't married. I still didn't know if I would marry him. I told him that everything always happened to us in July, and if everything goes the way it should, then I would probably marry him next July. I was testing him to see how he would react around Tom. To see if he was the man he said he was. The party was great everyone came, Joe took out the Karaoke and before long Tom and Joe were singing together. I was very happy and Tom was happy, this was meant to be. I said good-bye to my friend once again.

I would like to end the story here at the crossroads of my life. I wish I could end the story like the fairy tales we read as children— they lived happily ever after.

In my life I am convinced that Ellie doesn't get to live happily ever after. I have always thought: *5 ¾ of inch never getting to 5'1 inch!*

Maybe it's a case of "saying so makes it so" let's find out.

———————

CHAPTER SIXTEEN

HAPPILY NEVER AFTER

I had my family and my home—everything I had ever dreamed. Joe was caring and he loved his son as well as my daughters. When we sit down at night Dawn curls up beside Joe to watch television, while Joy and I always sit together. The first year was perfect. Joe was attentive, caring, and loving to us all. We were married in July, Lenny and Darlene were our witnesses. We all walked to City Hall and I remember on the way Darlene mentioned to me.

"Ellie, why aren't you nervous? Your big day is finally here."

"With Joe, getting married is just like a normal day, right Joe?" I asked.

"There's always a divorce or death," he answered, flippantly.

What he actually meant was that this was nothing but a piece of paper. It's funny how a marriage ruins a relationship. It only took two years and everything fell apart. His mother moved next door and his father contracted Alzheimer's. His mother was a horror, and we fought constantly. I liked his father a lot and I would protect him. I think they lived with us for less than a year. Joe and I fought constantly, one night I actually left him.

I won't go into specifics, let's just say on one holiday, after driving my Nanny back to the nursing home, we were in the car alone and I was feeling upset with his mother's actions earlier. I commented my feelings to Joe.

"I don't want to listen to this anymore!" he said abruptly.

"Well, maybe when I stab your mother 100 times, and there's blood all over my hands, maybe you'll listen to me then?" I quizzed him. He just looked at me.

"You know you're crazy right?" He pulled the car over and we finally talked. His mother moved out by March. She wasn't all to blame, but she certainly didn't help.

I gave this marriage all I could and soon it became hard financially. To help support Joe I started delivering newspapers, it was easy money and I could be home with my children. I did this for five years.

Joe was always depressed when we were alone, finances, commuting, every excuse he could find. If people were around he was a different man—funny, sociable, calling me honey, putting his arms around me. After three years of marriage, the man who was passionate and filled with love was no longer there.

He completely changed. When we were first together I remember him telling me.

"I never want you to do anything you don't want to." It was so sweet.

Well, he lied about that too. Sadly, to take it a step further, when we were together I refused to do certain things. We no longer made love, we just had sex, because he felt as a husband these were the things couples did. I would joke about it.

"Next you'll have me hanging from a chandelier," I laughed, trying to make light of it. Finally, I realized the soft, caring man that I saw years ago was yet another lie.

Basically, if I didn't do the things he liked, then we didn't do anything. The sin was he truly didn't care. He was like a roommate. In the beginning I was upset, but it was only sex, and we had a life together and a family. Julia was the only friend who I confided in. I was broken and didn't know what to do. Julia and I spoke about my options, but there weren't too many. Joe and I argued a lot, but we also had a lot of fun, one would outweigh the other.

I remember one night we were arguing, I wasn't happy and neither was he. I wanted to know why we should live this way?

We had different interests in everything. The only thing we had in common was our son, Brian, and marriage should not be based on the children alone. I told everyone throughout the years that I stayed in my marriage because I did not want my son to grow up without a father, but it wasn't the truth.

We had a big fight that evening, and I told him I was leaving. He acted very mean to me and threatened me with the custody of our son.

"He's my son and you are not going to win custody, you can't even take care of yourself, how the hell are you going take care of a child?" I screamed at him.

"I may not get custody, but I'll make damn sure that your son hates you," he replied. "Brian will know that you are nothing but a whore." He then threw up the past naming Sean, Winston and of course, Tom. He came right at my face and told me.

"I will make my son hate you." My whole life I had never been afraid of a man. Anytime a man even tried to raise his hand to me, I never backed down. I would tell them.

"Go ahead, you will be responsible for the consequences, because if you don't kill me, I will kill you."

This was different. The whole situation was mean and vindictive. He showed me that night he only cared about himself, he didn't seem to even care about Brian. To use our child to hurt me, really made me question what kind of a man I had married?

Mark was mean, but never like this, he never involved the girls in our problems. I was afraid. Joe was one of three children and one of this brother's kids hated their mother, I guess this was the family way. I changed that night. I didn't leave, but I did feel trapped. When I moved out of the projects I lost that financial security. I made the best of it, but I was never the same again.

Through the years I have done everything: delivered newspaper, faux painted homes, worked for Liz Claiborne painting in the malls. I worked for a company that owned a traveling clothing store. We went to nursing homes in the northeast region to sell clothes. I would work three months, and then be off the next three months. The job was hard driving the trucks to various locations, but I did have a lot fun. I had my own crew Michael, Joey and Rosie.

I would usually be gone no more than ten days at a time. I had a woman living in to keep up with the housework. Joe hated that job and did nothing to support me at all. Coming home after ten days a person usually misses you, not him, he was mad and couldn't appreciate the fact that I was helping support our family. It wasn't the greatest job, but I was off the entire summer and then from December to March.

The last year I worked for the company I made $55,000 for only working six months out of the year. Looking through my journal for that year, I saw how depressed I was. Joe had given me a hard time the night before I was to leave for another ten days, but surprisingly the next morning he tried to be nice by apologizing. He kissed me and mentioned that I smelled good. He wanted to know if it was new perfume.

He was about to hear a woman's scorn.

"No Joe, it's Channel # 5!" I yelled, "The only perfume I wear. I've worn this fragrance since I was seventeen-years-old. It's amazing after all these years you don't even know my perfume." I mocked a laugh, "what a joke this marriage is, what a joke you are. No, the joke is on me!" I turned, and left for my trip.

MY NANNY'S PASSING

The worse thing to happen that same year was when my Nanny died. I was busy traveling with the business and raising my children. Nanny had been living in a nursing home for the last four years, disabled from her third stroke. She was in a hospital and knew it was the end. I stayed with her all night in the hospital, and then they moved her back to the nursing home to hospice. I needed to work and had to leave her.

When I came home from work and made dinner, my mother called to say that Nanny was dying. I dropped the phone, ran out of the house, and drove straight to the nursing home crying my eyes out.

"Please Nanny, don't die before I say good-bye to you," I repeated over and over again. It usually took me forty-five minutes to get there. I made it in twenty minutes. I ran into the room and found my uncle and his girlfriend standing there. I held my Nanny in my arms, I kissed her and told her how much I loved her. I thanked her for loving me and kissed her on the forehead, my tears ran down onto her face. She took her last breath and died. The nurses came in and confirmed that she had passed.

"She waited for you, Ellie," said my uncle.

"I know. She knew I had to say good-bye to her," I acknowledged him.

I drove home that evening and truly wanted to die. How could I live without her in my life? I was lucky I had her for almost forty years. At her funeral service I had my niece read my poem:

MAGIC FLOWER

Our life is a beautiful garden
Where many seeds have been planted
Each flower grows alone
With vibrant colors and scents
Then emerges that one very special flower
That magical flower
This flower does not stand alone
The color not any brighter than the others
The scent not any stronger
Just one look and you see the magic
The flower's beauty is within
It carries a special love and warmth
To be shared by all
It spreads its love year after year
It is left untouched
So through the years
Each generation can see the magic
The magic is not in its beauty
The magic is not in its strength

The magic is love
The love this flower makes me see
The flower has shown kindness
It gives us warmth teaches us strength
It lets us see the beauty within ourselves
As the flower aged it never lost its magic or strength
Just one day the flower was gone
But the magic never left
I can no longer see this flower with my eyes
But just close them once
And then it appears in my heart and mind always

After the poem was read, I got up and spoke at her service:

"To me Nanny was this magical flower. I shared her love, warmth, and kindness to all. There is not a person in this room who has not felt her magic. She has touched our hearts in so many ways. Through the years we shared both the good and the bad of our lives with her. We are all so lucky to have known such a woman. Today we sit and cry for her loss, but tomorrow I will stand proud, knowing that I cared for her and she cared for me. What else could be said, but thank you! Thank you Nanny for all the magic and love you gave me through the years."

After Nanny died, I didn't speak to my family for five years. I left the job because it was too much of a hassle, what with Joe, and along with that my boss was unappreciative. I went to work for one of Joe's friends who was a doctor. He had an office in New Jersey. Within six months I was hired full time and started a medical billing company with him. He promised that we would be partners in the endeavor, which unfortunately never came to light. The first two years were probably the happiest I had been in years.

WAR OF THE ROSES

I was working again. No training, just thrown in there and within two months I was hiring seven new employees. We soon had to move to a larger office space. The first year we collected over five million dollars for our accounts. I was appreciated by my new boss and that was a new adventure, finally I felt Ellie was coming back. I have lost myself so many times in my life, but I guess that's what life is all about.

The girls graduated from high school, and Brian played sports, baseball, basketball, and later football. These were our fun years. Joe coached baseball and I worked the kitchen for the baseball league in our town. We always had people in the house, always entertaining.

For the first time in eight years I found a new friend. Rita came into my life and she truly made me laugh again. We both loved going to Atlantic City, but it was more than that. Over the years it seemed that the women who became my friends had no past, or if they did, they did not speak of it.

I remember Mary and I were friends for about three years. Vanessa had planned a jewelry party at her house and Mary came with me. At the party Vanessa and her girlfriends were telling stories about the past. In the car, on our way home, Mary said something very strange to me.

"I have to apologize to you. All the stories you have told about your life, I thought were lies. I cannot believe you did all those things," she said, bewildered.

"Why would I lie? That is what happened to me," I quickly told her.

This was when I realized that I was very different from her and the other girls in New Jersey. Rita was a breath of fresh air, she had a past and we loved to talk about her past situations. She would laugh when I shared mine. Her youngest son, Jeremy, was the same age as Brian. Finally, I had a friend and that made every day a little bit better. For my birthday she sent a singing telegram to my office. She was crazy, just like me.

I ran the kitchen for the baseball tournaments that summer and I had all my friends help out. All the guys were there to assist in sprucing up the place. I made a lot of friends. I started volunteering at a Women Homeless Shelter and Donna, Rita, Ronnie & Kelly would go with me. I started the annual Christmas

Party at the shelter. I also planned annual Christmas parties at my home. We had over sixty people coming to our home every year. These were my friends and I loved all of them. In a way they became my escape from my life with Joe.

It turned out that this would be the night Joe wanted to make love. I was exhausted after cooking for three days, entertaining until two in the morning, so maybe he picked that night because I was too tired to fight with him. We were always laughing with our friends. Joe and I were like Burns and Allen, they were the old comedy couple, only it was reverse with us—I was Burns and he was Allen. He would sing and I would do everything else. I didn't care I liked being busy and doing things. If I wasn't busy, I would be forced to truly look at my life with Joe. He was truly just a friend, he wasn't a husband who cared or loved me. Oh, he would buy me things, but usually for show. Everything with Joe was a show; his Cadillacs throughout the years and later his Corvette, all of which we could not afford. I would often wonder whom he was trying to impress. Did he really think people cared? Why did he feel that he had to be better than most people?

Joe also hated working. He complained everyday about something. Every morning he would wake up after ten hours of sleep and complain that he didn't sleep well. I had insomnia and felt lucky to get five hours of sleep a night. It was a challenge for me to stay motivated, so I made a point of going to work before he woke up.

Problems arose at the job and I quit. I started my own business out of the house. The first year was difficult, and admittedly there was not a lot of money coming in, but my marriage got worse. I missed not having an outlet to get out of the house. Joe constantly complained, it wore thin with the children and Dawn would get really mad. We couldn't wait for him to leave.

I had remained friends with Victoria, Lorraine and Sophie. We wanted to do a reunion with everyone from the real estate company. I honestly don't know what year it was maybe 2002 or 2003. I know it had been over ten years since we were together last.

Vanessa, Frannie, Lorraine, Victoria, Catherine, Sophia and Tom were invited. The night before the party Joe was in rare form, I was cooking and he came into the kitchen and announced.

"I can't believe you are doing this," he said antagonistically.

"What am I doing?" I asked, confused.

"I can't believe your inviting *that* man into my house."

"How do I have a real estate reunion and not have Tom here? Are you kidding me, after all these years? Please knock the shit off and stop. How would you feel if I was to invite Stella, that would be a smack in your face wouldn't it?" he said, sarcastically. "I wish Stella would come into your life again and you would leave me. That would make me so fucking happy!" I mocked.

"Are you going to get all dressed up tomorrow for your lover?" he continued. I was cutting up some vegetables and I had a very large knife in my hand. I looked at him, walked over to where he was standing and pointed the knife right in his face.

"If you embarrass me tomorrow, I promise you, I will cut your fucking throat!" I hissed, "Everyone coming here tomorrow are my friends. I refuse to go through this again with you, how many fucking years are you still going to be throwing him in my face?" I glared at him. "Joe, if you embarrass me, I will kill you. I have nothing to lose any longer. Sitting in a fucking prison would be a vacation, compared to living with you. Don't fuck with me because I am not kidding!" He turned away and walked upstairs. I had made my point.

The next day I was really nervous and at one time Tom came over to ask me if he could use the house phone. I saw Joe glaring at us.

"It's in kitchen," I pointed.

Normally, I would walk the person to the phone, but I was afraid to be alone with Tom. I don't know if Tom sensed my nervousness, but I avoided him all day. If was nice seeing everyone, and as usual Ellie and Joe represented the happily married couple. Ellie laughing as usual, no one would ever know. I don't know if Joe drank a lot that day, but that night he was terrible. He started an argument right after the last person left. I was happy and it bothered him. You see I wasn't allowed to be happy. I don't even know how he started the fight. We were loud and Dawn came in, she was trying to defend me and to stop the fight. I couldn't believe what he said.

"Do you think I'm wrong? I shouldn't be jealous that your mother has her boyfriend in my home?" He asked her.

"Stop it Joe, he was mommy's boss, it's nothing to get jealous over," Dawn said.

"Did you know that you mother slept with him? You don't know what your mother was like before I married her. S-she . . . " I didn't let him finish that sentence. I ran up the stairs and I started punching him and screaming.

"My daughter. My daughter, how could you say that to my daughter? You are fine meeting with Tom to get an appraisal for this house every time you want to refinance it, and you have no problem meeting him with Richard. You are not a man, you are scum. I never thought I could hate you more than I do."

I couldn't tell you how the fight ended. All I know is that I didn't speak to him for months.

After fifteen years of marriage the only vacation I ever had was in Florida, which we drove to because Joe wouldn't fly. Our vacation was with our son Brian, Joe's daughter and his grandchildren. That was my only vacation, no honeymoon, never anything with just the two of us. That was about to change.

LIFE GOES ON

I organized a vacation with two girlfriends. I went to the Cayman Islands with Ronnie and Kelly; we were acquaintances through the baseball club. We had a wonderful time and all agreed to vacation every two years together. We became great friends and met every available Friday for breakfast.

One day a friend asked me to run for council in my town. I didn't get a chance to accept, Joe did it for me. The job offered medical insurance, it didn't pay well, and it was a part-time job.

Only one meeting a week, and I would help out the community. I had to meet Louis he was running for mayor, and I would be on the ticket with him. We met at the football rally where I agreed that I would run. He told me what our platform would be and we went to the rally. All I had to do was introduce myself and ask for the vote.

That evening I was standing there with Louis, all dressed up, and the first person that came up to me said, "Ellie what are you doing?"

"I am running for Councilwoman."

"Get the fuck out of here," she joked.

Then I would introduce everyone I knew to Louis. He would go over our platform. After standing there for about an hour, we had over one hundred people come up to me. Louis was shocked that I knew so many people. What he didn't realize was that I had three children of different ages. Brian played sports, and I worked the baseball kitchen. So I did know a lot people. Earlier in our meeting he had mentioned that we needed to come up with a slogan. Another friend came up to me and said the same thing. Louis smiled, "I think our slogan should be "Get the fuck out of here." We laughed.

They set up a campaign meeting at Starbucks with a campaign consultant to run our campaign. He had previously refused to run it because he didn't like the people on the ticket and felt they wouldn't win. I didn't know this until we were at the meeting. I thought they had just dropped out. The first person I met was James, my running mate for Council, then Russell, he was the campaign manager, and of course my friend Dominick, the head of our town's Republican Club. Steven was sitting at the table and I was introduced to him. The man seemed crazy, but I shook his hand and sat down.

"Perfect, she's perfect," he repeated, and sat down to talk with me. He began throwing questions at me regarding my religion, my belief's, and volunteering. I answered all his questions. I just thought the man was totally insane. He loved that I was a registered Democrat. I was never a Democrat, but when I moved to

New Jersey some one knocked at my door and registered me as one. So this lunatic wanted to run an advertisement having me change my political affiliation. He talked about running the campaign around me, but Louis squashed the idea right away.

"Do you realize you have a diamond here?" Steven asked. "People are going to love that face, you have the Irish, you have the Italian, and you have the baseball and basketball communities. This woman volunteers in a children shelter, she is your diamond. I tell you what Louis, I will take the campaign now because she is going to win it for you."

He bent over and touched my face.

"Look at that face?" he questioned.

I looked at him in amazement and told Dominick he was insane. Well, from that moment on there was friction between Louis and I. The first fundraiser rolled around and it would be my first public appearance to announce that I was on the ticket. It was held in an exclusive catering hall, we would wear formal attire, Louis called me all day trying to prepare me for my speech.

I was so nervous, my girls took me to the mall to get my makeup done and get me out of the house. I got to the hall feeling confident that I looked good. I wore a black and white sequined dress. I was still a size two at the time and my hair and makeup was perfect. I rode up the escalator and Dominick was waiting at the top for me. He was in his tuxedo looking rather dashing. I was shaking and he walked towards me.

"You look absolutely beautiful," he grabbed my arm, "Are you ready?" he asked.

Then all of a sudden I started crying.

"Dom, I can't do this." Dom did not know what to do.

"Stay here I'm going to get Ronnie."

Ronnie arrived and took control.

"Stop this, you look so beautiful, your going to ruin your make up," she yelled.

"I can't do this. I can't speak in public. This isn't me!" Dom spoke up.

"How about we do this . . . we go in the room together, no announcements, you walk to your table and then when you feel comfortable, we'll start the speeches, okay?" he suggested.

I agreed and went into the room. There were some people that I knew, and it wasn't all that bad. Louis's speech was at least fifteen minutes long, then James spoke and his speech was five minutes. My time had arrived. I went to the microphone with an index card in my hand.

"Hello, my name is Ellie Connelly. I am running for councilwoman and would like your support. That's it! That is all I have to say, and I needed an index card for that? I thank you, please support us." I turned and sat down.

Then everyone in the room laughed and applauded me. Afterwards I felt like a bride at a wedding going to the tables, thanking everyone for attending, and hoping that they would support our cause. Louis and I were hard workers. We would pick a development weekly and knock on doors asking for their support. When we went to one particular development, Louis couldn't believe how many people knew me. I told him that I had delivered newspapers in that area for five years. We stood in front of supermarkets every weekend, in the evenings we had coffee at people's homes, and we held our campaign meetings. We had a full agenda.

I was never a public person and even a worse public speaker. At my debate I could see my children's faces and they were embarrassed. I sounded horrible, my voice was shaking, and the microphone had trouble picking up my deep voice. Thank God there were not a lot people there at the end of the night.

I called Tom and told him that I was running for office, and he told me that I was too nice for politics and shouldn't be doing it. I told him I would probably lose any way and that it was no big deal.

The night before the election all my friends called to support me and told me they voted for me. I remember telling one of them how embarrassed I would be tomorrow if I only got five votes.

"Tomorrow you will see how many friends you truly have," she told me.

We were at a pizzeria, our election night headquarters. Votes were coming in, and excitement filled the room awaiting the outcome. Then finally there was the announcement that we had won! This was truly a great moment in my life, not for winning the election, but looking at my children's faces, they were so proud of me. The guys carried me onto the table. I remember looking around at all the people who had supported us, but looking at their faces made me feel so proud. I secretly did wish Tom was there to share this moment. He would have been most proud of me. Tom did call the next day and he gave me his sympathy. He knew what I would be in for now. Through my years on council we spoke many times.

I found that I couldn't change completely, and all the professionals carried a bet that I would say, "fuck" in public. When I was council president, one resident would come to every meeting, and end up yelling at me. He was so angry. This particular night, I put my hand over the microphone, everyone thought I was finally going to say the F word, but instead I had some fun.

"Excuse me Jay?" I asked, "Did I ever date you and I just don't remember?"

"No," he answered, with a surprised look.

"I just wanted to make sure, because you are so angry with me. I've only seen this kind of anger from men I dated," I said. "I just wanted to be sure." I gave him a big smile. Everyone on the dais and audience began laughing.

I must add that I won the bet, and believe it or not, I never said "fuck" in public while I was on the Council for the four years.

Those years were the most chaotic of my life. Joy got married. It was a beautiful wedding and reception. Joe sang "All the Way" for their first dance. It was a magnificent evening, my daughter was so happy and they are truly soul mates even today. I'll skip two years and jump to my last year in my term on Council.

Brian was in his senior year in high school, and my daughter Joy surprised me with the news that she was going to have a baby. I was so excited, now I was going to be a grandmother. Becky had called me a few months earlier from Florida. She also was going to be a grandmother. We were very excited, and through all these years we had remained friends, but about a month later she called me to tell that she had cancer. I was devastated. She didn't want me to come down until after her treatment ended, and then wanted us to go somewhere together when she felt better.

She never did get better, her Aunt called and told me she was in hospice, it wasn't even three months. I flew out the next day, I met her husband for the first time, we talked all night, he told me that she wouldn't know who I was because she was so heavily medicated. When she finally woke he stroked her hair and let her know I was there.

"It's Ellie from New York." He said to her.

"I know," she answered.

"I think she thinks you are the other Ellie who takes care of her," said her husband.

"No, I know who the fuck she is, it's fucking Ellie!" she said, "T-tony . . . T-tony . . . Tony . . . " she repeated over and over remembering. Then she grabbed my hand. I started crying and she said to me.

"I'm fucking dying, Ellie."

"I know, I fucking hate this, how am I going to live without my friend? You're the only one who ever got me." I told her. We were both crying and hugging each other.

"We had fun and I love you," she told me, and I sobbed.

"I love you. Becky. I am going to miss you so much."

I flew home. She died the next day. I was so angry at Joe because a few years back when she was marrying her second husband she wanted me to be the matron of honor, and Joe wouldn't let me go. He told me that I didn't know her anymore that she was marrying a man called Pancho, and besides we didn't have the money. I will regret not being there for her until the day I die. Her son had a baby girl, and Joy had a boy. They were born three months apart. It would have been nice to share this next chapter of my life with Becky. I turned fifty and was asked to run for higher office, but I declined because of my business.

My family threw me a surprise 50th birthday party. All my friends and family attended, and at the party my girlfriend Camille (who has three children of her own) commented to me how lucky I was to a have such a loving family. She mentioned that we don't see this anymore, children who truly love their mother.

Joe sang "All the Way" to me. There were a few lines in the song that I reacted too like, *through the thick and thin years, and all the in between years, come what may.*

"Come what may," I yelled out to him.

Joe laughed, and kept singing.

Everyone in that room had heard Joe sing me that song through the years. They truly believed that this was a man who loved me. Joe sang the song, but he never felt the words, it means nothing to me now. It was my song, years before I had told Joe about the song and how much it meant to me. I had told him that if I would ever marry again that's how I wanted it to be—all the way. I have seen through the years this was yet another deception of Joe's. This was truly the last happy evening that I shared with all my family and friends.

CHAPTER SEVENTEEN

———— ❧ ————

HUMILITY – ADVERSITY – TRAGEDY

I n 2008 I lost the election for my second term. Brian was back in college after the Christmas break, and I felt such a void in my life. No more rushing around, no phone calls needing to be made, it was just dull and boring. I tried many times in the previous month to find something that Joe and I could enjoy together. He was still miserable, and with Brian away he cared about nothing. He was offered a job singing at a bar in Staten Island, but he wouldn't take the job. This made no sense to me because every week he would go out on his Karaoke nights and sing for pure enjoyment with all his friends. If he sang just one night, it would pay for Brian's student loan, and we could have a social life again, but he refused to see my reasoning and logic.

Everyone could see how unhappy I was. My daughter Joy wanted me to move to South Carolina and wanted me to leave Joe.

"You could take your business with you," she began, "there is no reason for you to live like this any longer, and mom . . . you are too young and vibrant to live this way," she pleaded.

I went to South Carolina, without Joe, for a vacation to see if we would like living there. It was nice, but it wasn't for me. Frankly, I had not made a decision if I was going to leave Joe. The Saturday night I returned from our vacation he was sitting on the couch watching television (as usual) so I went into the family room to ask him a question.

"Joe, let's do something together tonight?" he shook his head to mean, no. After all these months of watching him pouting I couldn't take it anymore.

"I am not doing this anymore," I blurted, "I can't live like this. I'm young and you are not going to make me into an old lady," I cried, "if you want to grow old and miserable, than that's fine, but I refuse to live the rest of my life watching television on this couch until you die."

"All you do is nag me," he replied. "Can't I get some peace in my own home?" he asked, turning up the volume on the TV. This infuriated me and I screamed back at him.

"I'm going to leave, you are miserable. I'm miserable, and can't live this way," I started in on him, "Yes, you are right, I nag. I've threatened to leave you numerous times throughout the years, and you don't take me seriously, but tonight? This is it!" I threw a pillow at him.

Brian wasn't at home and there was so reason for me to stay. He started screaming that I was never satisfied with anything, and I always wanted more.

"What? What do I want more of? I moved into your home that you bought with someone else. I've done nothing but support you financially and emotionally."

"You've done nothing, nothing that any other wife does," he replied.

"You bastard! Take a look around at the other wives, our friends' wives? You tell me if you can name one woman who has come close to doing anything that I have done through these years," I challenged.

"It's always you, always you," he whined.

"No Joe," I said, "just the opposite, it has always been you! You are the man, not me, you were supposed to take care of me, love me, and you didn't," my voice was trembling. "We don't have sex anymore, would you like me to tell all our friends and family how you truly are?" he remained silent and just kept shaking his head as I continued. "You have no problem pointing out my faults to everyone. I know I'm not perfect and I have never claimed to be."

"For Christ's sake Ellie, shut the fuck up!" he said, turning away from me in his chair, but I kept pouring out my hurt and hate onto him.

"You know all I ever wanted was for you to love me, and you couldn't do it," I began crying.

Usually when I got this upset he apologizes, calms me down and it gets forgotten. I don't know why everything happened next, maybe he knew that I was really leaving this time and wanted to be as mean as possible. He couldn't hold Brian over my head any longer. I don't know and never will understand what came out of his mouth next.

"I never loved you the way you wanted me to because I didn't! You always knew that!" He told me in such a stone cold manner. I knew he was speaking the truth.

"Then tell me why? Why did you come back so many times, and why the fuck did you marry me?"

"Because you were pregnant and I wanted a family," he answered.

"You didn't have to marry me you cocksucker. I was fine having the baby on my own," I yelled back.

"I know, and that is why I knew you wouldn't marry me if you knew the truth," he told me casually. "I wanted to raise my son, and if meant staying with you, well that was the price I would have to pay," those words cut me like a knife.

I had always thought I could never be hurt anymore from this man, but I was wrong. He tried to justify what he said by making me wrong, and of course then he started in on Tom.

"Ellie, why do you think you are any different then me? Who is calling the kettle black? You did the same thing all these years, you loved Tom and you settled for me," he hissed.

"Are you fucking crazy? A person I spent one night with, you are going to throw that in my face nineteen years later?"

"No," he said, "it wasn't just that one night, it's the way you felt about Tom, he was perfect, smart, and he was caring, remember?" He was blabbering.

"No! No! No!" I screamed. I could feel the veins on my neck protruding. "From the day we made our commitment to each other there was never anyone else. I gave you everything, and you gave me nothing back. You had given it all to Stella, so don't bring Tom into this, you have no right."

The pain and anger I felt was overwhelming me, I wanted to hurt him back.

"Yes, Tom was everything in so many ways, but I knew that he didn't love me, and I accepted that. The reason why you bring up Tom's name is to hurt me, why is it that you don't throw Winston's name in my face, which you should because I cheated on you with him.

"Winston loved me, but you know you can't hurt me by bringing up his name. You make fun of the song Lady In Red when it comes on the radio, and that should hurt you knowing someone loved me that much. I don't hear you bringing up Mark's name, why? I don't regret that night with Tom, and you read something you had no right to. It killed you to hear how he made me feel."

We continued screaming at each other, and it was like playing a game of ping-pong. As long as one of us kept picking up the racket it continued. Boy, we were really clearing the air this time. Hashing out the same old shit!

I needed to calm down so I walked into the kitchen to get a glass of water. My hands were trembling, and I was so angry and mad at him, knowing that I had wasted nineteen years on this piece of shit. I quickly got myself together and went back in there. I was surprised to find he had turned off the TV

"So Joe? Remember the first time we had sex and you told me you never wanted to do anything I was not comfortable with? Huh,

huh?" I provoked him, because I was going to rub his face in that promise.

"You were a fucking liar! Through the years you tried things in that bedroom taking it a step further each time until I never wanted to be with you anymore. You took all my feelings away. It's been four years since we have been together sexually, and before that maybe once or twice a year. I heard every excuse in the world, why can't you just be honest and tell me that I'm not Stella!"

He got up from the couch, took my face in his hands, and stared deep into my eyes.

"You are not Stella! Yes, I loved her! Yes, she hurt me! Yes, I never loved anyone the way I loved her!" He screamed loudly, spitting all over me. Then he pushed my face away.

"Thank you. Thank you for finally being honest. I just need to know why, why me, why did you have to keep coming back into my life?" Joe stood up and pretended to be straightening the cushions. He found it difficult to look at me.

"In the beginning it was the challenge and the passion. Then I knew you were the kind of person who would take care of me and love me. I know you are going to leave me now that Brian is gone. There's no reason for you to stay with me. We have done enough to one another," he said, and sat back down on the couch.

I went upstairs to my bedroom and revisited everything that was said. I knew this was the end. The weeks went by and I didn't feel upset, it was a relief to know that I was finally going to be free. It wasn't something I could do overnight, I had my business in the home. I felt no emotion and there was no need to leave immediately. It did not matter if it took a few months, I had been here this long, and now at least I knew I was leaving. It's funny I blocked out most of what Joe said that night, and I didn't remember until three years later.

TRAGEDY STRIKES

On April 30, 2008 Joe left for work. About 1 p.m. the phone rang and Joe's secretary was screaming,

"Joe is having a stroke."

I rushed to the hospital where I was told he had a massive stroke. He had a blood clot in his brain and within a few hours they were doing brain surgery. When people say your life can change in an instant, this is so true.

After the operation, Joe woke up and I discovered that he had no speech and was paralyzed on his right side. The doctors kept insisting for me to sign a DNR (Do Not Resuscitate), but I refused. I protected him and fought with all the doctors to have him rehabilitated. He was angry and violent, the only way I could calm him down was to lay in bed with him. It was so sad, he needed me and I was the only person that made him feel safe.

Everyone saw how much Joe needed me, so the next few months I was running to hospitals and rehabilitation to get him well enough to come home. These months are a blur. All I remember is fighting for him, protecting him and loving him. He had no disability insurance, I couldn't make the mortgage payments and I even tried fixing up the house so I could sell it, but the market crashed.

I thought we owed about $250,000 on the house, but we really owed $430,000. I had nothing and on top of that I had a disabled husband coming home to a house that would soon be foreclosed on. All these years I had worked, now to lose everything! I was in better shape in the projects. Brian came home from college the night of his father's stroke and then he wanted to return. I was against it. I felt he should stay home and go to the local college for the next semester. Joe had only come back from the nursing home a few days before. Yes, I was afraid to be alone with Joe, but that was not the reason. I didn't want Brian to go away to college. I knew what I was going through, and Brian had to face the reality that the father he had known was gone. When someone dies you grieve, but there comes a time where you expect to move on. This was not the case. Joe was here in the flesh, but the Joe we knew was gone.

Brian needed this time to mourn and accept it and I felt by leaving it allowed him to escape.

I was trying to persuade him not to go back to college. I didn't have the money for car repairs and all I saw was Brian running away from this life. The day he picked up his car, his attitude really bothered me. All he seemed to be worried about was where to put his new speakers, unfortunately with all the stress, I lost it and started screaming.

"You are not going. Brian, I can't handle this. You are not being responsible, you can't go back to that college, you have to stay here and that's it!" I told him firmly.

"It's not fair, you are ridiculous!" Brian screamed back at me.

Dawn came out screaming at me. What came out of their mouths was basically that I was a selfish human being who didn't do anything for any of them their whole lives. I was a terrible mother and did nothing for them. Then I realized that everything in my life must have been a lie.

"It's all about you," Dawn said and Brian agreed. Joy was there and she just listened to everything. Not attacking me, but yet not defending me either. I remember running out of the house that day with my disabled husband, I could hardly breathe I drove to the school parking lot and cried like I've never cried before.

I felt like I was truly a disgusting human being, and just didn't see it. I must have lived in a fantasy world. No matter who I loved, even my own children couldn't love me back. I still can't write or think about all the disgusting things they said to me that day. I remember sitting in the car with Joe thinking and going over all the years. I had stayed for fear of Joe's threat that Brian would hate me. Now I see they all hated me, was all of this for nothing? I was so unhappy with Joe that I didn't give my children what they needed. Could it be all the things Joe had said to them through the years that had turned them against me?

Then the words kept repeating in my ears.

"It's all about you," they had said. "It's all about you."

In the last eighteen years nothing has been about me. I didn't have a fancy home, jewelry, clothes, and vacations, like all the things my friends had. I thought I had a family and that meant more to me than anything. Now I had found a new hurt, a hole in my heart that can never be mended. Brian left and went back to college and as the months went by I was barely holding on.

Christmas came and I did my annual Christmas party, all our friends came. I thought it would make me feel better, but I got more depressed. It wasn't the same and I started to go into a deep depression. Joy made me an appointment with a therapist and I started seeing her weekly, but this was different. I was no longer the young girl who could change her future.

I had a disabled husband who openly admitted a few months before that he never loved me. I was planning on leaving him, and now I'm taking care of him for the rest of his life. My children had told me how they despised me. No therapist could fix that. Yes, it was good to talk to someone without every word that came out my mouth being twisted by someone. It was too hard living in this house with the memories and waiting to be foreclosed on. Our friends didn't come around any longer and the phone calls had completely stopped.

Surprisingly, at this time, Stella came into my life. Her girlfriend Gail would call every week concerned about Joe. Finally, I gave in, what did it matter now?

"Tell Stella to call me," I told Gail.

She really loved Joe and hated what had happened to him. We were so much alike. It may shock you, but she was the person who gave me strength to make my next move. She sent me vitamins to take care of myself, and we talked every evening. She knew I needed somebody. Our friendship started, but we never talked about the past, only the future. I told her my life story and she told me hers. I never brought up the supposed cancer scare that she had, and their engagement, for what?

GHOSTS IN THE CLOSET

My relationship with Dawn grew worse every day. She hated me and I saw it every time she looked at me. We argued almost every day, she was beating me down and just when you think you can't be beaten down anymore—the answer is yes you can!

When you think nothing else can be taken from you, there is always one more hurt to be had. One day Dawn and I were arguing about me moving to my father's house in Pennsylvania. My girls wanted me to move to Florida. Why would I move to Florida? I hate the heat. Why would I want to move so far away from my family and friends?

Dawn became out of control over something, and stormed out of the house. A few minutes later she came back in and threw a piece of paper at me.

"Here, this is for the perfect mother!" she announced bitterly.

I opened the piece of paper and read what she had written, my stomach immediately turned.

"Your father molested me when I was twelve!"

I could feel my heart beating out of my chest, and my throat was closing. This was horrible, every parent's worst nightmare. What made it even more unbearable was that it was my father. I called my therapist and scheduled an appointment with her because I wanted to make sure I handled this the right way. I did not want to hurt Dawn. I wanted to kill my father. I still do, and that will never go away. That was my baby and he abused her. I will hate him every day of his life. If there is a hell he should burn every day over and over again.

Dawn was engaged and was planning her wedding. She made me promise that I would not confront my father. As hard as it was I agreed and tried to be there for her, have her go to counseling. We got close for a little while, but it didn't last. I told my mother because I had no one to talk to and she told the family, so of course it was my entire fault. I should have never told my mother. Then the insanity started within my family not believing Dawn, it was an extremely hard time for all of us. My family split, my sister and her children, and my brother Mikie believed my father. My brother, Nicky, and my mother were the only ones who believed Dawn.

I haven't spoken to any of them since that day and I never will. Through therapy I learned that Dawn would always blame me for not protecting her, which she has the right to do. I did not protect her, and it was my job. In her eyes I will always be the person that wasn't there for her. It's a shame, I found cards that Dawn had made me through the years and in each card she would write how much she loved me, she used to call me Super Mom! She admired that I was pretty, hardworking, tired, and I was always there for her. What happens to families? How quickly things can change. My father has hurt me more than he ever did in my childhood. He took my daughter's innocence, not to mention her love and trust away from me.

Stella was my friend through all this turmoil and showed me that I had to leave. She found a home in Florida with a builder who would hold my mortgage, so I could take my business. She assisted me financially; it allowed me to make the move. She would be living in the same development.

I went to Tom's office before I left. I wanted to thank him for doing the appraisal on my home for the bankruptcy. I made up a wine basket, and planned to drop it off before an appointment I had with one of my accounts. I thought it was his day off, I could do this without seeing him, but he was there. I told him that I moving and how optimistic I was about that move, and how it would be good for Joe and me.

He looked happy, he had remarried for the third time, and I believe he found his true love. I didn't stay very long, we hugged each other, but I knew that this was truly the last time that I would see him. I did write him a note thanking him, not only for being there but for the past and how he had helped me grow as a person.

Dawn had her wedding, it was a beautiful day and she was very happy. She married a man who truly loved her. That's really all a parent wants for her child, isn't it? We did get together at the house to watch Dawn's wedding video, but that would be the last time we were together in our home. Joy moved in June to South Florida, and I moved in July. Leaving the home was the hardest of all. I had raised my family there. I planted my flowers each May, and I did not know how to say goodbye to this life and home. I still don't.

———————

CHAPTER EIGHTEEN

MY AWAKENING

I moved to Florida, depressed and alone. One of employees moved down with me to keep the business going. Stella moved down three months later. I thought at least I would have a friend. We really did not have anything in common, except for Joe. She lived in the past and every time they were together she would go down memory lane with him. She felt it was good to talk about their past relationship. Joe couldn't talk, and we didn't know what he fully understood. Joe would laugh with her, he looked forward to her coming to our home, and that I had to be thankful for.

One day I had an appointment and left Joe at Stella's house. When I returned there were pictures scattered all over her table, pictures of her and Joe. I felt uncomfortable, given what I had been through with this man. I had to sit there as she showed me pictures of their life together. Not a great time.

It was the end of December and that meant my birthday. I thought I would be spending it with either my son or daughter, but neither one came. Stella made birthday plans at a restaurant with music, but she doesn't dance and neither did Joe, he can't!

I sat there patiently watching other people dance and having fun. Joe has partial aphasia, but then to my shock he got up from sitting next to me and sat by Stella. He proceeded to put his arm around her all night and kept trying to touch her boobs. They were both laughing like little children. I could not believe that I was sitting there watching this man behave so inappropriately. Finally, a man came to our table and asked me to dance. Joe waved him on to dance with me. I was truly humiliated. The man was extremely nice and became most upset when I explained that Joe was my husband.

I came home that night and tried to figure out which was the worst day in my life, at this point there had been so many. This was ridiculous and I had put myself in this situation! In June, Stella and I had a long awaited argument and I never called her again. This was the end of that strange friendship. It was not healthy for either one of us. I did not need the daily reminder of the love they shared, and the pain it had ultimately caused me.

I had never experienced true loneliness until now, living in the Bible belt I really don't fit in. Everyone says: *God Bless you, the lord be with you!* One person actually gave me a wooden cross at a restaurant where I was dining saying: *God is watching the care you give this man and you will be rewarded.* I just looked at the person and thanked him. I was thinking, *"Get the fuck away from me."* I'd rather hear just one person say, "Go fuck yourself!" I would feel a little bit more at home.

I still smoke and I am a pariah of sorts in this new world of health freaks.

I still curse, and when I do I see the people offended by my words. I try not to curse, but it comes natural. I don't curse to be mean. In my family growing up it was a normal way of expressing myself, and that is hard to change.

I tried looking for a hobby or a sport:

First I tried shooting, I went to a gun range, had my thirty minutes of instruction, and now I know how to shoot a gun. My instructor told me what to shoot at and I did. When he pulled in my paper he was surprised to see how well I had done. He went on to say that I was an expert shooter and really didn't need lessons. I tried it, and it was okay, but I got no enjoyment out of shooting.

Secondly, I thought I might take flying lessons, but I suffer with vertigo. The flight instructor advised me that it wasn't such a great idea for me to even think I could fly a plane with vertigo.

Thirdly, I tried horseback riding. After two rides I was told that I was a natural, but I didn't like it. The horse galloping at full speed just wasn't for me.

I found myself calling Tom one day to tell him about my lessons. I realized that over the years, I looked for reasons to call him. I can't explain why, but I needed to know that he was all right. Our conversations never lasted long. I may not call him for three or four years, however this call was different. He was nice and polite as usual but something had changed. He laughed at my story, but what I heard was pity in his voice for me. When I hung up the phone I felt like it was a bother for him to talk to me. I had never felt that before.

I decided not to call him again and wondered if that might be our last conversation. I realized he never called me and through the years, it had always been my doing the calling. I tried to hold on to the memory of our friendship and that's exactly what it was—a memory.

The following October, I experienced another loss. Matty was coming down to see me and thinking of relocating. He planned to stay with me for a while. But only three days before the date on his airline ticket, I was notified that he had died. I took his death the hardest, but channeled my loss into writing a beautiful eulogy for him. My friend Danny read it during the service. A few of the guys from high school came to the service. I was able to catch up with a lot of my old friends. It was great seeing them. Jimmy and I talked the longest. I punched him in the arm jokingly.

"That was for my wedding," he just laughed. He knew he was wrong many years ago. It was sad that because of Matty dying, I was able to get to see my old friends. Everyone goes in different directions and I guess that is life.

Over the years we make new friends, but there are some you can never replace. For me these special friends are: Danny, Becky and Matty. They really got me, and showed me unconditional love. They saw all of me and still loved me, how great is that?

It has been almost two years since Matty's passing and I still can't say his name without crying. My daughters lost an uncle and I lost my oldest friend, we miss him every day. Dawn had a baby girl and I know that Matty is watching over her.

My friend, Julia, who had been diagnosed with breast cancer five years prior, received some bad news over the next few months. She was told that the cancer returned and she had to have a double mastectomy. She went through a really hard time, and I hated being so far away from her. I don't think I could lose another friend, we talked regularly and I made her laugh. I told her that she had to beat this cancer thing because I needed her. I began to feel like I was out living all my friends. I didn't want that, it hurt too much to live with all the memories, and have no one to share them with. I wanted to share my memories with people who experienced them with me.

2014 was our 40th year high school reunion. I couldn't even think about going. Not to have Matty there to share our stories would be devastating, and not to see others I had known, I wouldn't do well so I decided not to go.

It has now been four years that I have lived away from everyone I have ever known. Dawn has her family and they live in New Jersey. Joy and Brian live almost four hours away. I try to go at least once a year to see my friends. So now here I am! I have lived an extra-ordinary life to find myself alone with Joe. I am without my children, my grandchildren and without my friends. My whole life I had feelings of being alone and unloved, and now it has resonated despite all the people who shared in my life.

This week I called over sixteen friends and not one person had the time to really talk with me. They do send little text messages like:

Thinking of you
Hope you are feeling better
Will call you when I have time
Just wanted to say hi

I know they care about me, but they really can't do anything for me. I understand, especially during the summer, everyone is busy. To make matters worse it is this digital world we live in. Verbal communication is almost extinct. The little text messages are the extent we have time for in this crazy, busy, and impersonal world of the 21st century.

I live every day to survive, every one tells me that I have to do something like, move back to New Jersey, move to South Florida and find happiness. Why? Apparently what made me happy didn't make anyone else happy. For a while I thought I was part of a family and I realize now it was just part of my fantasy. The only person who was happy it seems sometimes was Ellie. I live with those memories and I cherish them. I have moments with my children and grandchildren, but I am not part of their lives. I feel like a visitor, someone they occasionally see and call. I'm not feeling sorry for myself—I am trying to understand life.

Does everyone have this in his or her lives?

Does everyone try so hard to be happy or loved?

I am only fifty-seven and sometimes I wish I were ninety, knowing the end would be coming soon. I'm tired of taking care of Joe, working for a future just to survive is unfulfilling. When I talk about the crossroads of my life, it may have been only four of my fifty-seven years, but in all those other years the people and the memories will last me until the day I die.

I guess the question I keep asking, is how can I find happiness again? What would make me happy? I've tried to find that one special man to share a life more than once, and I failed. I found what I thought was a soul mate, but I was wrong. I had my children and raised them, not as well as I probably should have. If I had been happier in my life, maybe I would have been a better mother. Now, all of them are happy with their families, and that's the way is should be. I do find happiness when I am with them, but how do I find happiness without them? How do I wake every day and not have a dream? My whole life I was able to dream, and now I just don't know what to dream about. I guess I need to live in that question.

I can't keep living in the past. Everyone is tired of the stories, even me. So I find myself writing and making the story of my life into a book in the hope that someone would enjoy reading about my life and my experiences. Maybe see a little of themselves and not feel so isolated. So they could feel connected to something or someone again. I don't know what the future will be throwing at me. I'm still strong, but I'm numb and I want to live again, I just don't know how? Once again, I want to live in that question!

CONCLUSION

I will wait for my Awakening and I will learn how to live again. I trust that something will awaken inside of me. I will feel happiness and laughter again. I'm done with tears and sadness in this life.

Friends suggested I write my story and I have. What an accomplishment! My children may never understand, I have told our story and they were part of the story. I am not ashamed of the life I have lived. I have named my special girlfriends in my dedication. They encouraged me to finally do something for myself without fear or conviction. They knew that years ago I started writing and how it seemed to free me. Now I have found that writing this book has been cathartic and it is healing my wounds and pain.

Tomorrow I will write another story, which will be a fantasy, and in this story there will be a happy ending because it won't be about me.

Sitting here reviewing my words for the ending of my book, I hear the phone ringing. I pick it up and there is a Lionel Ritchie song playing on the other end of phone:

> We lost what we both had
> You know we let each other down
> I do love you
> Still . . .

Listening to the song, tears of joy roll down my cheeks. I feel myself awaken within. As the song ends his voice says:

"Ellie do you know who this is?" As soon as he said my name, I knew who it was. I smiled and answered. YES!

THE END FOR NOW